THE BEGGAR'S OPERA

Born in 1685, JOHN GAY was apprenticed to a silk mercer in London for a short time before returning to his family in Devon where he began to write verse: *The Shepherd's Week* (1714) was his first major success. In 1711 he came to the attention of Alexander Pope and the Scriblerus circle, and this friendship was of crucial importance to Gay, who produced most of his later work in this ambience. Seeking a regular income, he became secretary first to the Duchess of Monmouth in 1712, then to the Earl of Clarendon in 1714. Thereafter he lived much in the houses of patrons, especially the Duke of Queensberry, whose wife was his particular champion. In 1727 he published his *Fables*, which ran to fifty editions by 1800 and assured his reputation as a poet for the rest of the century. *The Beggar's Opera* was first performed in 1728 and, with its witty combination of political and social satire, traditional songs and parody of Italian opera, was an immediate theatrical triumph. It was followed by *Polly*, which was banned by Walpole and consequently also became a financial success. Gay's other writing includes the libretti for Handel's *Acis and Galatea* and *Achilles*. A popular and genial man, Gay was always beset by financial difficulties. For example, in 1720 he invested in the South Sea scheme when the market was at its height, only to lose much of his money when the bubble burst. He died in 1732 in the Queensberrys' house and was buried in Westminster Abbey beneath his own epitaph:

> Life is a jest, and all things show it,
> I thought it once, and now I know it.

BRYAN LOUGHREY is Research Director at Roehampton Institute. He has also edited Izaak Walton's *Compleat Angler* and, with Neil Taylor, *Thomas Middleton: Five Plays* for the Penguin Classics.

T. O. TREADWELL is senior lecturer in English at Roehampton Institute. He has contributed to a number of scholarly journals.

JOHN GAY

THE
BEGGAR'S OPERA

EDITED BY
BRYAN LOUGHREY AND T. O. TREADWELL

PENGUIN BOOKS

PENGUIN BOOKS

Published by the Penguin Group
Penguin Books Ltd, 27 Wrights Lane, London W8 5TZ, England
Penguin Books USA Inc., 375 Hudson Street, New York, New York 10014, USA
Penguin Books Australia Ltd, Ringwood, Victoria, Australia
Penguin Books Canada Ltd, 10 Alcorn Avenue, Toronto, Ontario, Canada M4V 3B2
Penguin Books (NZ) Ltd, 182–190 Wairau Road, Auckland 10, New Zealand

Penguin Books Ltd, Registered Offices: Harmondsworth, Middlesex, England

This edition first published 1986
13 15 17 19 20 18 16 14 12

Set in Palatino Linotron
Printed in England by Clays Ltd, St Ives plc

CONTENTS

INTRODUCTION

The Beggar's Opera is one of the great success stories in the history of the London stage. The original production which opened at the playhouse in Lincoln's Inn Fields on 29 January 1728 ran for sixty-two performances in the first season, smashing all previous records, and for the rest of the eighteenth century it was performed more often than any other play;[1] it has been revived regularly ever since, as well as having fathered a host of imitations, adaptations and parodies, one of which, Brecht's *Threepenny Opera*, is a major work in its own right. The characters of *The Beggar's Opera* passed into the mythology of its age as the characters of Dickens were to do in the next century – when, for example, the young Boswell goes to a tavern with two girls he has picked up, Gay's lyrics and Gay's hero come naturally to his mind: 'I surveyed my seraglio and found them both good subjects for amorous play. I toyed with them and drank about and sung *Youth's the Season* [II.iv] and thought myself Captain Macheath.'[2] For more than two hundred and fifty years *The Beggar's Opera* has had a permanent place in the cultural repertory of the world, and this in itself is likely to blind us to the aspect of the play that most impressed and delighted its first audiences – its originality.

The originality of *The Beggar's Opera* is implicit in its title, which to an audience in 1728 would have seemed a striking contradiction in terms.[3] 'Opera', to an audience in the 1720s,

1. See William Eben Schultz, *Gay's 'Beggar's Opera': Its Content, History and Influence* (New Haven, Connecticut, 1923), p. xxi.

2. *Boswell's London Journal, 1762–1763*, edited by Frederick A. Pottle (London, 1950), p. 264. In a note to an earlier passage, Pottle comments that 'In one way or another the figure of Macheath dominates this entire journal' (p. 252).

3. This point is well made by Peter E. Lewis, 'The Uncertainty Principle in *The Beggar's Opera*', *Durham University Journal*, 72 (1980), 143.

meant the Italian opera which had first appeared in London in 1705 and which had been much in vogue ever since. Songs, of course, had been common on the English stage since Tudor times, and by the latter part of the seventeenth century plays containing within them masque-scenes in which the dialogue was sung rather than spoken had become fashionable and were called operas. The Italian opera took this development further and eliminated spoken dialogue altogether, the passages between the various arias being carried on in recitative. The novelty of this was stressed by Addison in *The Spectator* for 3 April 1711, one of the many numbers of this very popular and influential periodical in which operas are discussed:

There is nothing that has more startled our *English* Audience, than the *Italian Recitativo* at its first Entrance upon the Stage. People were wonderfully surprized to hear Generals singing the Word of Command, and Ladies delivering Messages in Musick. Our Countrymen could not forebear laughing when they heard a Lover chanting out a Billet-doux, and even the Superscription of a Letter set to a Tune.[4]

Early numbers of *The Spectator* return again and again to the triviality and absurdity of the Italian operas of the day, but no amount of ridicule could dent the popularity of the form – seventy-five years after its first appearance in England, Dr Johnson was to write resignedly of Italian opera as 'an exotick and irrational entertainment, which has been always combated and always has prevailed'.[5] Eighteenth-century opera audiences *liked* the exotic and were quite prepared to take an evening's holiday from common-sense; they must also have enjoyed the music, which, especially after the arrival of Handel in London in 1710, was superior to anything that had been heard on the London stage, at least since the death of

4. *The Spectator*, edited by Donald F. Bond, 5 vols. (Oxford, 1965), I, 119–20.
5. Samuel Johnson, *Lives of the English Poets*, edited by George Birkbeck Hill, 3 vols. (Oxford, 1905), II, 160.

Purcell. Italian singers were imported and lionized, especially those sensational prodigies the *castrati*, whose peculiar condition was as fascinating as their vocal skills.

As well as being musically novel, the Italian operas that enraptured fashionable London in the first decades of the eighteenth century were remarkable for the sumptuousness of the costumes and the sophistication of the stage machinery. The libretto of Handel's very popular opera *Rinaldo* (1711), for example, requires the heroine to be carried through the air in Act I in a 'Chariot drawn by two huge Dragons, out of whose Mouths issue Fire and Smoke', while Act II calls for waterfalls as well as 'Thunder, Lightning, and amazing Noises'. With so much spectacle to engage its attention, the audience at an opera was unlikely to concern itself greatly with the details of the plot, which was in nearly every case if not manifestly absurd at least considerably remote from the concerns of the everyday. The opera plots of the period regularly take their subjects from myth, legend or ancient history. The characters, invariably high-born though frequently required by circumstance to disguise themselves as slaves, suffer heroically for love or are impelled by its inexorable force to acts of the blackest villainy, but goodness triumphs at last, as does the spirit of forgiveness, and a happy ending is somehow wrenched out of the confusion.

It was not the plots but the spectacle and, above all, the singers that brought fashionable London to the Italian opera. The Royal Academy of Music was founded in 1719 specifically 'for the Encouragement of Operas', and the Academy sent Handel himself to Italy to recruit the best available artists. In 1721 the great castrato Senesino was lured to London and in 1723 he was joined by the famous soprano Francesca Cuzzoni; both were paid what was in those days the fabulous sum of £2,000 for the season.

A second celebrated soprano, Faustina Bordoni (always called simply 'Faustina'), arrived in 1726. She was paid £2,500, even more than Cuzzoni, and a jealous rivalry between the two ladies erupted almost immediately. The three great Italian singers were first brought together on the London stage in May 1726 in Handel's *Alessandro*, an opera carefully constructed so that neither Cuzzoni nor Faustina could claim to have the better role. The story concerns two women, Rossana (Faustina) and Lisana (Cuzzoni), both in love with Alexander the Great (Senesino); he wavers indecisively between them for virtually the whole length of the opera, only choosing Rossana at the last possible moment before the final curtain. This even-handedness did not prevent the rivalry between Cuzzoni and Faustina from becoming notorious, however, and the London opera public divided into opposing claques so enthusiastically that by the spring of 1727 the young Lord Hervey was complaining that nobody talked about anything else.[6] Matters came to a violent if farcical head at a performance of Bononcini's *Astyanax* in June 1727 in which both Cuzzoni and Faustina appeared. Showing scant respect for the Princess of Wales, who was present, the rival partisans in the audience became restive and then violent; as a contemporary newspaper reported, 'the Contention at first was only carried on by Hissing on one Side, and Clapping on the other; but proceeded at length to Catcalls, and other great Indecencies'.[7] Spurred on no doubt by the excitement, Cuzzoni and Faustina so far forgot professional decorum as to come to blows on the stage, and the performance was abandoned in confusion.

John Gay regarded the Italian opera craze with a sardonic eye. In a letter to his friend Jonathan Swift dated 3 February 1723, he wrote:

As for the reigning Amusement of the town, tis entirely Musick, real fiddles, Bass Viols and Hautboys not poetical Harps, Lyres, and

---

6. See *Lord Hervey and His Friends, 1726–38*, edited by the Earl of Ilchester (London, 1950), pp. 18–19.

7. *The British Journal*, 10 June 1727, p. 3.

reeds. Theres nobody allow'd to say I sing but an Eunuch or an Italian Woman. Every body is grown now as great a judge of Musick as they were in your time of Poetry, and folks that could not distinguish one tune from another now daily dispute about the different Styles of Hendel, Bononcini, and Attillio. People have now forgot Homer, and Virgil & Caesar, or at least they have lost their ranks, for in London and Westminster in all polite conversation's Senesino is daily voted to be the greatest man that ever liv'd.[8]

Underlying this sarcasm is a fear (shared by other dramatists, including Addison, who expressed it in number eighteen of *The Spectator*) that the popularity of this affected foreign music would drive the true English drama off the stage, and Gay's own 'opera', when he came to write it in 1727, begins by mocking the conventions of the Italian form. The Beggar–Author explains to the Player that he has 'introduced the similes that are in all your celebrated operas: the swallow, the moth, the bee, the ship, the flower, etc. Besides, I have a prison scene which the ladies always reckon charmingly pathetic' (Introduction). The 'Simile Aria' was a characteristic feature of heroic opera in the Italian style, and Gay fulfils the Beggar's promise; 'the swallow, the moth, the bee, the ship, the flower' duly appear in, respectively, Airs thirty-four, four, fifteen, ten, and six. Prison scenes are indeed very frequent in operas of the period – Handel's *Floridante* (1721) and *Tamerlano* (1724) both have one, for example, while the eighteenth-century historian of music Sir John Hawkins saw Macheath in Newgate as a parody of the prison scene in an opera called *Coriolanus* by Attilio Ariosti, first performed in London in 1723.[9]

'As to the parts,' the Beggar continues, 'I have observed such a nice impartiality to our two ladies, that it is impossible

8. *The Letters of John Gay*, edited by C. F. Burgess (Oxford, 1966), p. 43.

9. Sir John Hawkins, *A General History of the Science and Practice of Music*, 5 vols. (London, 1776), v, 315.

for either of them to take offence' (Introduction). This had been Handel's policy in *Alessandro*, and the original audience had no trouble connecting the Beggar's words with the Cuzzoni–Faustina rivalry, still the talk of the town in January 1728. This connection made, the quarrel scenes between Polly and Lucy take on an extra comic significance as reflections of the jealous contention in the opera world – as in Handel's opera, the hero makes his choice between the two ladies only at the very end. The language in these scenes, particularly Lucy's soliloquy and air at the beginning of Act III, scene VII, has a marked 'operatic' quality, and the rats-bane in Polly's gin parodies the device of the poisoned cup which makes a frequent appearance in Italian opera plots.

The Beggar asks to be pardoned for the fact that his opera, unlike all of the others, is not 'throughout unnatural' (Introduction). This is, of course, a satiric dig at the remote and high-flown world of Italian opera and is reinforced at the end when, despite all the claims of narrative logic and poetic justice, the Player insists that Macheath be reprieved because 'an opera must end happily', and the Beggar acquiesces on the grounds that, 'in this kind of drama, 'tis no matter how absurdly things are brought about' (III.xvi).

Gay's work, then, has a complex relationship to the modish opera of the 1720s. In part it parodies it, with its lack of concern for the 'natural', with its simile arias, its solos, duets, trios and choruses, and with its rival heroines who quarrel on stage. But *The Beggar's Opera* is more than a parody of the conventions of opera; it is an inversion of them, an anti-opera offering us, instead of the floridly baroque arias of Scarlatti or Handel, English and Irish folk songs; instead of the royal palace or the enchanted island, the alehouse and the prison; instead of heroes and goddesses, thieves and whores.

Compared to the airy confections of the Italian opera, the world of Gay's comedy is grittily real. The contemporary London in which *The Beggar's Opera* is set was a society radically divided between the extremes of poverty and wealth. The metropolis was growing rapidly out from its medieval centre within the city walls, the expansion being mostly to the west, where the prevailing wind gave the prosperous classes some relief from what the political economist Sir William Petty, writing in 1662, called 'the fumes, steams, and stinks of the whole Easterly Pyle'.[10] In the early part of the eighteenth century, the gentry were moving from the old fashionable quarters of St Giles, Covent Garden and Soho into the new developments to the west. Hanover Square began to be built in 1719, the first stage in what was essentially a huge new town between the lines of what are now Regent Street and Park Lane, built to house London's wealthiest citizens and the tradesmen who supplied them with the luxuries the fashionable life required.[11]

As the rich moved to the new western suburbs, the parts of London that they vacated became progressively disreputable. The population of the metropolis was increasing, and the consequent demand for cheap housing meant that fortunes could be made in speculative development at the bottom end of the market. Existing structures were expanded and new buildings run up wherever space permitted, uncontrolled by planning restrictions and without the slightest regard for the provision of adequate light or sanitation, so that the poorer quarters of London were warrens of filthy alleys and narrow, dark courtyards bordered by ramshackle tenements known as 'rookeries', crammed from cellar to garret with tenants paying a rent of a shilling or eighteen pence a week.

The readiest relief from the squalor of life in places like these was through alcohol, and between about 1720 and 1751 an epidemic of spirit drinking swept through the slums of London. The misery of life in the rookeries would doubtless have

10. *A Treatise of Taxes & Contributions* (London, 1662), p. 23.

11. See Hugh Phillips, *Mid-Georgian London: A Topographical and Social Survey of Central and Western London about 1750* (London, 1964), pp. 243–58.

fostered drunkenness under any circumstances, but from about 1710 onwards the situation was exacerbated by an official policy to encourage the newly developed distilling industry, which provided both a source of revenue for the government and a new market for farmers at a time when the price of grain was low, and which soon came to be regarded as essential to the prosperity of Britain.[12] Everything was done to promote the new industry; the price of its products, of which gin was the most important, was kept very low to encourage the widest possible consumption and the trade was completely unrestricted; anyone who could pay the low excise duty was free to distil spirits and once distilled they could be sold without even the licence required of alehouse-keepers.

The results were catastrophic. In the slum quarter of St Giles, where, the Beggar tells us, his opera has often been performed (Introduction), more than one house in every four was a gin shop by 1750.[13] Most of the gin shops were also brothels of the cheapest kind and places where stolen goods were received, embodiments of a vicious spiral of drunkenness, degradation and crime. Hogarth's famous print *Gin Lane* (1751), which is set in St Giles, is so horrifying that we assume it to be a caricature, but the scenes of brutal depravity which it depicts are documented over and over again in the records of the period. M. Dorothy George cites the pathetic case of Judith Dufour, who took her two-year-old child out from the workhouse where it was lodged one afternoon in 1734. The child had just been given new clothes, and for the sake of these Judith Dufour strangled it, leaving the body in a ditch in Bethnal Green. She sold the clothes, for which she received the sum of one and fourpence, and spent the money on gin.[14]

12. A typical view is that of Daniel Defoe, writing in his journal *The Review*: 'the Distilling of Corn is one of the most essential things to support the Landed Interest that any branch of Trade can help us to, and therefore especially to be Preserved and Tenderly used' (9 May 1713, p. 186).

13. See M. Dorothy George, *London Life in the Eighteenth Century* (London, 1951), p. 41.

14. George, p. 42.

The dark courtyards and tortuous alleyways of the older and poorer quarters of early eighteenth-century London were, not surprisingly, dangerous as well as squalid. In a pamphlet published in 1751, the lawyer and novelist Henry Fielding remarked that:

Whoever indeed considers the Cities of *London* and *Westminster*, with the late vast Additions of their Suburbs; the great Irregularity of their Buildings, the immense Number of Lanes, Alleys, Courts and Bye-places; must think, that, had they been intended for the very Purpose of Concealment, they could scarce have been better contrived. Upon such a View, the whole appears as a vast Wood or Forest, in which a Thief may harbour with as great Security, as wild Beasts do in the desarts of *Africa* or *Arabia*.[15]

Fielding's simile is telling; the slums of London were a jungle which the well-dressed and respectable explored at their peril. In 1730 the tradesmen of Covent Garden complained to the magistrates that, 'Several people of the most notorious characters and infamously wicked lives and conversation have of late . . . years taken up their abode in the parish . . . There are frequent outcries in the night, fighting, robberies and all sorts of debaucheries committed by them all night long.'[16] It was said that a well-dressed man couldn't walk from the Piazza of Covent Garden to the Rose Tavern, a distance of about fifty yards, without risking his life twice.

If we remember the brutalizing combination of poverty, filthy living conditions and widespread alcoholism, we will not be surprised that crime was endemic in the London slums, but at the time of *The Beggar's Opera* this was exacerbated by the chaotic and ineffectual system for policing the metropolis which had developed haphazardly over the centuries. By Gay's time responsibility for maintaining law and order was shared partly by the Justices of the Peace, assisted by their officers the Constables, partly by the High Constables (whose

15. *An Enquiry into the Causes of the Late Increase of Robbers* (London, 1751), p. 76.
16. Quoted by George, p. 83.

duties were rather vague), partly by the Beadles and the Watch, partly by the King's Messengers, together with various bodies of men under the Sheriffs, and partly by the City Marshalls. The Constables, Beadles and Watch had severely limited powers of arrest and could not function outside their precinct boundaries except by permission of the neighbouring Constables.

Not only was this system cumbersome and redundant, it was also hopelessly corrupt. This was because virtually every permanent official involved in the administration of London, from the City Recorder downward, had to buy his place. This had long been recognized as a serious evil, but as there was no money to pay adequate salaries there seemed no alternative to it, and it was not until Victorian times that the sale of offices was brought under control and eliminated. The cost of official places was high. At the time Gay was writing *The Beggar's Opera*, for example, the price of the post of Keeper of Newgate Prison was £5,000 (about £100,000 in today's terms) and the man who laid out so large a sum for his position felt entitled to recoup his investment by any means whatever. Thus it came about that a cell in the Press Yard at Newgate, regarded as the most desirable part of the prison because it offered a little light and fresh air, was one of the most expensive rooms in London; for the privilege of lodging here, a prisoner paid a deposit of £500 plus a weekly rent of twenty-two shillings, excluding 'garnish', the system of tips to guards and fellow-prisoners demanded by custom. Gay's Macheath is speaking without exaggeration when he complains on his entrance to Newgate that, 'The fees here are so many, and so exorbitant, that few fortunes can bear the expense of getting off handsomely, or of dying like a gentleman' (II.VII).

The enforcement of law in eighteenth-century London was obviously inefficient and corrupt and the only response the authorities could make to what appeared to be a rising tide of crime was to increase the savagery of the punishment meted out to those who were caught and convicted. The law's most effective instrument was considered to be terror of the gallows. Between about 1680 and 1722, the number of offences punishable by death was increased from eighty or so to over three hundred and fifty.[17] Thefts became capital when the amount stolen was one shilling or more from a person, five shillings or more from a shop, or forty shillings or more from a house, but smaller thefts became hanging offences if they were carried out with menaces; breaking and entering was always capital, as was any theft committed between sunset and dawn.

However draconian these measures now seem, fear of the rope appears to have had little effect on the crime rate, and the authorities, powerless to enforce the laws they had, responded by creating new ones. In 1706 an act was passed which for the first time made the receiving of stolen goods a capital offence. This act also contained a section encouraging criminals who were prepared to inform on their accomplices; if the evidence led to conviction, the informer received not only a free pardon but a reward of forty pounds. The intention behind this act was to break up the gangs of thieves by encouraging them to betray one another, but its real effect was to bring into being a class of professional informers, called 'thief-catchers' or 'thief-takers', who operated by perjuring themselves and blackmailing their victims, often young men and women who had taken up crime against their will in the first place. A letter printed in the *British Journal* for 1 May 1725 gives a detailed description of the system in operation. The anonymous correspondent describes his conversation with a young thief called Morris Evans:

17. Paradoxically, the annual number of criminals actually executed in the eighteenth century was lower on average than it had been in Stuart times; this is because the judges had wide powers of pardon which they exercised very frequently. It has been argued that this was a deliberate tactic designed to increase popular awe at the majestic authority of the judicial system; see Douglas Hay, 'Property, Authority and the Criminal Law', in *Albion's Fatal Tree: Crime and Society in Eighteenth-Century England*, edited by Douglas Hay and others (London, 1975), pp. 40–49.

Upon my perswading him to leave off robbing, he said it was impossible, (except he banished himself, which he now thought to do:) For, said he, the Thief-Catchers are our absolute Masters . . . and they send us into several Wards and Stations, (as a Corporal sends Soldiers to stand Centinel;) and if we refuse to go, they'll immediately have us committed for some former Crime; or . . . bring Evidence to swear away our Lives wrongfully. He told me there was at that Time, six Thief-Catchers that he knew, and where they kept their nightly Clubs, to which if their Gangs did not repair, they were in Danger; and from thence they must go whereever they sent them. He said the Thief-Catchers went every Morning to all the Prisons, to see[k] for new Offenders; where they ask'd them their Case, and taught them how to plead; and if they had Money, would find some such Contrivance, as in our Case, to bring them off; and whichever Thief-Catcher came first to such new Offender, he must be his Slave for ever after, and rob when he bid him, or be hang'd for refusing . . . And he said the Thief-Catchers, and Buyers of stolen Goods, were become, in a Manner, Joint-Partners; and had Warehouses in obscure Places, both in the Town and Country, where they kept some Things a Year before they durst expose them to Sale.

As Morris Evans's story shows, the system of offering rewards for the conviction of felons offered enormous power to those clever and unscrupulous enough to exploit it. No one grasped the opportunity more successfully than the man who remains the most famous criminal of the period, the self-styled 'Thief-Taker General of Great Britain and Ireland', Jonathan Wild.

Wild was born in Wolverhampton in 1683, the son of a carpenter, and moved to London as a young man.[18] His early career in the capital is obscure, but he associated with criminals and spent some time in prison. By 1714, with the assistance of an extremely corrupt City Marshall called Charles Hitchen,[19]

18. For Wild's life and criminal system, see Gerald Howson, *Thief-Taker General: The Rise and Fall of Jonathan Wild* (London, 1970). This excellent biography provides the best account of the London underworld at the time of *The Beggar's Opera*.

19. Hitchen was a cabinet-maker who bought his place as Under Marshall for about £700 in January 1712 and immediately began recouping his investment by blackmailing

Wild had turned to the twin trades of thief-taker and receiver and was making himself master of the London underworld. His system was brilliantly simple: Wild would get at one member of a gang of thieves and persuade him to inform against two others, then find a fourth to accuse the first in case he became dangerous – not only did this technique soon put the whole gang in his power, but the forty pound reward was payable every time. Having taken control of the gangs, Wild could send them out to rob to his orders; as poor Morris Evans's testimony suggests, individual thieves were helpless in the thief-taker's grasp.

This was a relatively old technique; where Wild improved on it was by moving *inside* the law and setting himself up as a public benefactor. He advertised widely in the newspapers to the effect that anyone who had been so unfortunate as to have been robbed might come to what he called his Lost Property Office in the Old Bailey. There he would settle a fee for the return of the stolen property, usually from one third to one half of its value, which was far more than an ordinary receiver would be prepared to offer the thief, especially now that receiving was a capital offence. The client would be asked to return in a day or two, at which time the 'lost property' would be returned by an anonymous hand reaching through a panel in the office wall.

The brilliance of this system was that Wild transferred all the risk to the thieves themselves. He never actually held the stolen property and so could not be accused of receiving it. His thieves provided a ready supply of goods for the Lost Property Office, and the rewards from the public financed further thefts. Thief-taking prevented the thieves from disposing of their loot to anyone but Wild, ensured his control over the underworld, brought in forty pounds a time, and earned the

criminals and dealing in stolen goods. For a summary of his career, see Donald Rumbelow, *I Spy Blue: The Police and Crime in the City of London from Elizabeth I to Victoria* (London, 1971), pp. 60–75.

goodwill of the public, to whom Wild represented himself, not without justification, as the only power capable of bringing criminals to justice efficiently. He did so ruthlessly. Gerald Howson, Wild's best biographer, calculates that the number of men and women hanged, transported, branded, imprisoned or fined as a result of being impeached by him between 1714 and 1724 was between 120 and 150.[20]

Wild's ruthlessness, cunning and energy made him absolute master of the London underworld, and to these qualities he added a genius for publicity. By 1720 he was a famous public figure; his agents were everywhere in Britain and his comings and goings were widely reported in the newspapers. But, as Howson suggests, the attitude of the respectable public towards Wild was mixed.[21] He seemed to be the one man who was really able to deal with crime in a practical and efficient way, though he did this entirely unofficially, unconstrained by the statutes that limited the authority of Constables, Sheriffs and City Marshalls, and besides this he was a charismatic and colourful figure. On the other hand it was widely recognized that Wild himself was a coarse and brutal man, that his associates were villains, and that his wealth and success were gained by methods that didn't bear looking into too closely. The Thief-Taker General had a certain tawdry glamour, but he was generally regarded as a figure of fun and when, in 1724, he finally overreached himself and was hanged for the offence of receiving a reward for the return of goods which he knew to have been stolen, few tears were shed. Wild appears frequently in the writing of the time, almost always in a comic or satiric context, and he is now best remembered as the ironic 'hero' of Fielding's *Jonathan Wild, the Great* (1743) and in his comic apotheosis as Peachum in *The Beggar's Opera*.

Peachum's name reminds us that, like Wild, his trade is to impeach or inform upon his criminal acquaintance for the sake

20. Howson, pp. 306–11.
21. Howson, pp. 124–8.

of the reward (the verb 'to peach' meaning to inform against or betray was current in slang use from Shakespeare's time until our own century[22]). Peachum's soliloquy in Act I scene iii in which he weighs up the members of his gang, deciding who shall hang immediately and who shall be spared to thieve a while longer, is likely to strike audiences as a moment of pure comedy, but it is also a precise reflection of Wild's method; in the same way, the scenes showing the partnership between Peachum and Lockit (II.x; III.v–vi) reflect the collaboration between Wild and the corrupt forces of authority which was so necessary to the thief-taker's success. Like Wild, Peachum operates both within and without the boundaries of the law; as a bringer of criminals to justice, he is the servant of the 'respectable' society on which he preys in his other role as the master of thieves. Wild and Peachum share a seedy surface respectability which masks their unscrupulous crookedness, and the cynical hypocrisy of this position is brilliantly exploited by Gay as he places the figure of the thief-taker at the centre of The Beggar's Opera, using Wild's career as the governing metaphor for his vision of the society of his time.

The Beggar's Opera was composed in the autumn of 1727 at precisely the time when Gay's long-cherished hopes of achieving financial security through a place at court had come to a disappointed end.[23] He had been born in Barnstaple, North Devon, in 1685. His parents belonged to the provincial gentry but were not particularly well-off, and in any case Gay was a younger son; he received the best education available in Barnstaple, but otherwise had his own way to make in the world.

The society of eighteenth-century England was run on a vast

22. As we might expect, the verb is used frequently in The Beggar's Opera. Mrs Peachum declares, for example, 'Ay, husband, now you have nicked the matter. To have him peached is the only thing could ever make me forgive her' (I.x).

23. The standard authority for Gay's life remains W. H. Irving, John Gay: Favorite of the Wits (Durham, North Carolina, 1940).

and complex system of patronage. The rich and powerful had control over a large number of more-or-less well-paid positions both in Church and State, and these they disposed of as their interests or inclinations led; many of these positions included in turn the power to dispose of other, lesser, positions, so that the system extended the whole way down the social scale until it reached the level of the labouring poor. For a young man with energy and talent but without independent wealth, the patronage system offered the only realistic means of advancement, and Gay, like thousands of his contemporaries, devoted most of his life to working it.

In 1707, when he was twenty-two, Gay came to London and took a post as secretary to his boyhood friend Aaron Hill, a wealthy and well-connected young man who was able to introduce his protégé to a circle of influential people in the capital. Hill helped Gay to publish his first important poem, *Wine*, in 1708, and his patronage opened the door to friendship with many of the most important writers of the day, including Addison and Steele. By 1711 or 1712, Gay had met the young Alexander Pope (nearly three years his junior) and the two formed what was to be a life-long friendship; in 1712 they collaborated on a volume called *Miscellaneous Poems and Translations* which contained the first version of Pope's *Rape of the Lock*. Gay's own reputation as a writer was also becoming established; his poem *Rural Sports* was published in January 1713 and a play, *The Wife of Bath*, was performed the following May. By the end of the same year, Gay had composed his brilliant set of mock pastorals, *The Shepherd's Week*, and by the beginning of 1714 he was a member of the Scriblerus Club, a group of young literary wits including Pope and Swift which was centred around the Tory politician Lord Oxford.

The wits of the Scriblerus Club were intimately associated with the Tory government, but the Tories fell from power at the death of Queen Anne in the summer of 1714 and Gay's hopes of advancement through political patronage collapsed;

his old friends were now powerless to help him and the newly triumphant Whigs regarded him as an enemy. Gay had some hopes of his friendship with the new King's daughter-in-law, Princess Caroline, the Princess of Wales, but these came to nothing and no place at court was offered to him.

Gay's literary career continued to flourish. The year 1716 saw the publication of his most ambitious poem yet, the mock-georgic *Trivia, or the Art of Walking the Streets of London*, and the production of a play, *Three Hours after Marriage*, on which he had collaborated with his fellow-Scriblerians Pope and Dr Arbuthnot. Both works were successful and profitable, but neither provided long-term financial security. This did seem to have been achieved in 1720, when the publication of Gay's *Poems on Several Occasions* earned its author the comfortable sum of £1,000, but Gay was unable to resist the speculative fever which was sweeping England at the time. He invested most of his money in South Sea Company stock, and when the South Sea bubble burst the bulk of Gay's fortune went with it.

Gay's hopes of patronage waxed again in 1721, when the political tide appeared to be moving in favour of his old friend Sir William Pulteney, but the real power lay in the hands of Sir Robert Walpole, who was revealing himself to be the master politician of the age and who had long distrusted Gay's Tory inclinations; Gay had to wait until 1723 to receive even a minor post, a commissionership of state lotteries worth £150 a year – at least a steady income, if a less-than-magnificent one. Gay's chief difficulty was that his principal friend at court was the Prince of Wales's mistress, Mrs Howard; the Princess of Wales, Princess Caroline, remained outwardly friendly to Gay, but she kept her husband under efficient control and was, moreover, an ally of Walpole's, so that the voice of Mrs Howard was unlikely to be influential when it came to filling vacancies in the royal household.

Gay himself must have been aware of this, and by 1725 he seems to have decided to try another tactic. Princess Caroline

had a four-year-old son, Prince William Augustus, and Gay
began writing a series of verse fables for him; these were
finished by the end of 1726 and published in March 1727. The
Fables were an immediate and long-lasting success (there have
been over 350 editions and the work has been translated into
virtually every European language), and Gay must have
thought that his hopes for preferment were at last to be
realized, especially after 11 June 1727, when George I died and
Princess Caroline became Queen of England. But Walpole's
hold over the government was as strong as ever, and when the
new list of court appointments was published in October, Gay,
after years of flattery and intrigue, was offered only the post of
gentleman usher to the two-year-old Princess Louisa, worth
£150 a year. Bitterly, he refused it.

The sardonic vision of contemporary society offered in *The
Beggar's Opera* must have its roots in Gay's sense of the system
that had demanded so many years of demeaning servility and
then withheld its reward, but the form in which this vision is
expressed, an ironic opera with a cast of rogues and whores,
had probably been taking shape in Gay's mind for some time
before the summer of 1727. Eleven years earlier, after *The
Shepherd's Week* had brought Gay fame as a pastoral satirist,
Swift had written to Pope suggesting that 'a sett of Quaker-
pastorals might succeed, if our friend Gay could fancy it . . . Or
what think you of a Newgate pastoral, among the whores and
thieves there?'[24] but there is no direct evidence that this hint
was ever communicated to Gay, much less that it provided the
germ of *The Beggar's Opera*.[25] More significant is a letter written
by Gay to his patroness Mrs Howard in August 1723, a time
when Walpole's power was fast increasing (earlier that year he

---

24. *The Correspondence of Jonathan Swift*, edited by Harold Williams, 5 vols. (Oxford,
1963–5), II, 215 (30 August 1716).

25. If Gay responded to Swift's suggestion, the most likely result is his poem 'The
Espousal', published in *Poems on Several Occasions* (1720), which takes up the idea of a
Quaker pastoral. See Irving, pp. 142–3, 235.

had forced Gay's friend Bishop Atterbury into exile), and Jonathan Wild's thief-taking career was at its height. Gay observes: 'I cannot indeed wonder that the Talents requisite for a great Statesman are so scarce in the world since so many of those who possess them are every month cut off in the prime of their Age at the Old-Bailey.'[26] The idea was further developed the next year, having been given impetus by a particularly sensational incident in the career of Jonathan Wild. On 14 October 1724, as a result of information provided by Wild, a thief called Blueskin Blake was brought to trial at the Old Bailey. Before the sessions began, Wild, who was mingling with the prisoners waiting to be tried, imprudently wandered too close to Blake, who seized him round the neck and attempted to cut his throat with a penknife. The knife was blunt, Wild survived the wound and Blueskin Blake was duly hanged, but the event caught Gay's imagination and his ballad 'Newgate's Garland' appeared in print before the end of the year. At the time the poem was written, Gay seems to have thought that Blueskin's murderous attack on Wild had been successful, but what makes 'Newgate's Garland' interesting is its author's association of the criminal milieu of Blueskin and Wild with more general levels of corruption and rogues in higher places. After two opening stanzas describing Blueskin's attack, Gay widens the theme; now that Wild has been removed, common criminals will be as free to exercise their trade as great ones have always been:

> Some say there are Courtiers of highest Renown,
> Who steal the King's Gold, and leave him but a Crown,
> Some say there are Peers, and some Parliament Men,
> Who meet once a year to rob Courtiers again.
>> Let them all take their Swing,
>> To pillage the King,
>> And get a Blue Ribbon instead of a String.

26. *Letters of John Gay*, p. 45.

Now Blueskin's *sharp Penknife hath set you at Ease,*
And Every man round me may rob, if he please.

Knaves of Old, to hide Guilt, by their cunning Inventions,
Call'd Briberies Grants, and – plain Robberies Pensions;
Physicians and Lawyers (who take their Degrees
To be Learned Rogues) call'd their Pilfering – Fees;
         Since this happy Day,
         Now ev'ry Man may
         Rob (as safe as in Office) upon the High-way.
For Blueskin's *sharp Penknife, &c . . .*

Some, by publick Revenues, which pass'd through their Hands,
Have purchas'd clean Houses, and bought dirty Lands,
Some to steal from a Charity think it no Sin,
Which, at home (says the Proverb) does always begin;
         But, if ever you be
         Assign'd a Trustee,
         Treat not Orphans like Masters of the Chancery,
But take the High-Way, and more honestly seise,
For every Man round me may rob, if he please . . .[27]

The view proposed in the last stanza, that the highwayman is at least frankly criminal and therefore more honest than those whose robberies are cloaked in respectability, is echoed everywhere in *The Beggar's Opera.* Peachum announces the theme in the opening song, '. . . And the statesman, because he's so great,/Thinks his trade as honest as mine' (I.i). The first audiences responded delightedly to this level of satire, particularly to the series of thrusts that seemed to be directed at Sir Robert Walpole, whose enemies were growing in number as his power increased. Among the members of Peachum's gang we find 'Robin of Bagshot, alias Gorgon, alias Bluff Bob, alias Carbuncle, alias Bob Booty' (I.iii); this was immediately

27. *John Gay: Poetry and Prose,* edited by Vinton A. Dearing with the assistance of Charles E. Beckwith, 2 vols. (Oxford, 1974), I, 288–9.

understood to refer to Walpole, whose opponents constantly claimed that he was enriching himself at his country's expense, and the name 'Bob Booty' was to stick to him for the rest of his career. Walpole was, allegedly, of an amorous disposition and *The Beggar's Opera* was seen to reflect this aspect of his character. Peachum complains to his wife that Bob Booty is unreliable because, 'he spends his life among women' (I.iv), and Macheath's inability to choose between Polly and Lucy, as expressed in the lyric 'How happy could I be with either,/Were t'other dear charmer away' (II.xiii), was widely taken to be an allusion to the triangular relationship between Walpole, his wife, and Maria Skerrett, his mistress.

Topical satiric allusion was seen in the quarrel scene between Peachum and Lockit (II.x), which was taken to refer to the deteriorating relationship between Walpole and his close political ally Lord Townshend, who was also his brother-in-law. Peachum and Lockit call each other 'brother' ten times in the course of this short scene, and Peachum's admonition that, 'we must punctually pay our spies, or we shall have no information' (II.x) may glance at the army of agents and informers that Walpole kept active, both at home and abroad. The quarrel reaches its climax when Peachum and Lockit seize each other by the throat, and there is some evidence that Walpole and Townshend's relationship so far degenerated that on one occasion they, too, attempted to throttle one another, though this episode seems to have taken place after the first performance of *The Beggar's Opera*.[28]

Whether or not Gay intended these moments of topical political satire, it is clear that his contemporaries received them as such.[29] But the satiric vision that shapes 'Newgate's

28. See Jean B. Kern, 'A Note on *The Beggar's Opera*', *Philological Quarterly*, 17 (1938), 411–13.

29. For a detailed account of contemporary response to the political satire in the play, see Schultz, *Gay's 'Beggar's Opera'*, pp. 178–97. See also C. F. Burgess, 'Political Satire: John Gay's *The Beggar's Opera*', *The Midwest Quarterly*, 6 (1965), 265–76.

Garland' and that expresses itself in *The Beggar's Opera* from Peachum's opening song to the Beggar's closing words is much more general and much grimmer than this. It reaches its climax at the comedy's darkest moment when Macheath, in the condemned hold in Newgate and facing the prospect of immediate execution, meditates on a society in which the very mechanism of justice is unjust, one in which criminal behaviour is virtually universal but in which only the poor are punished for it. Gay brilliantly intensifies the irony of Macheath's vision by having him express it in a song to the tune of the Elizabethan love lament 'Greensleeves'; the gentleness and courtesy of an older age evoked by the melody clashes starkly with the bitter words Macheath sings to it:

> *Since laws were made for every degree,*
> *To curb vice in others, as well as me,*
> *I wonder we han't better company,*
> > *Upon Tyburn Tree!*
> *But gold from law can take out the sting;*
> *And if rich men like us were to swing,*
> *'Twould thin the land, such numbers to string*
> > *Upon Tyburn Tree!*
>
> > > (III.xiii)

For a play which is so often regarded as a period romp, *The Beggar's Opera* takes a remarkably dark view of human nature. It has at its centre the Polly–Lucy–Macheath love triangle, but this is set beside the intensely cynical view of courtship and marriage expressed at regular intervals throughout the play by the elder Peachums and Lockit.[30] The love-plot is drained of any tinge of romance: Lucy is pregnant, as she announces in

---

30. A particularly good example comes from Mrs Peachum: 'If she had had only an intrigue [i.e. a love-affair] with the fellow, why the very best families have excused and huddled up a frailty of that sort. 'Tis marriage, husband, that makes it a blemish' (I.ix). This inversion of conventional moral values is characteristic of the play.

the first speech we hear from her (II.ix), and Macheath's heroic protestations of undying love for Polly in I.xiii are declared to be a sham by Macheath himself in II.iii, while II.iv shows him dallying amorously among the whores. As for the hero's courage, it lasts only as long as his brandy holds out (III.xv). The criminal world is no worse than the world of respectable society, but it is no better either; Macheath is betrayed, with a Judas-kiss, by his former lover Jenny Diver and later by Jemmy Twitcher, a member of his own gang. Lockit, in a remarkable passage, regards himself as bound by the principles of human nature to cheat his partner Peachum:

Lions, wolves, and vultures don't live together in herds, droves or flocks. Of all animals of prey, man is the only sociable one. Every one of us preys upon his neighbour, and yet we herd together. Peachum is my companion, my friend – according to the custom of the world, indeed, he may quote thousands of precedents for cheating me. And shall not I make use of the privilege of friendship to make him a return? (III.ii)

The cheerful ending of *The Beggar's Opera* is achieved only because the Player insists that 'an opera must end happily' in order to comply with 'the taste of the town' (III.xvi). He overrules the Beggar's intention to end the piece in conformity with the principles of 'strict poetical justice' (III.xvi), which would require the hanging of most of the characters and the transportation of the rest. Poetic justice, the requirement that virtuous characters be rewarded and wicked ones punished, was taken very seriously in neoclassical drama because it was seen to reflect the fundamentally just nature of God's universe. Gay gives his Beggar–Author a final speech in which he expresses yet again the play's principal theme, the equivalence between the overtly criminal behaviour of its characters and the proceedings of the respectable world. The Beggar concludes:

Had the play remained, as I at first intended, it would have carried a
most excellent moral. 'Twould have shown that the lower sort of
people have their vices in a degree as well as the rich: *and that they are
punished for them.* (III.xvi)

The irony of the last words (the italics are ours) subjects the
idea of poetic justice to the test of a real world where justice is a
commodity and where moral values are a function of wealth
and power. The tavern and prison milieu of *The Beggar's Opera*
exposes by contrast the exquisite opera-world of high romantic
loves and suffering nobly born; in the same way, Gay's cast of
rogues and whores presents his vision of the squalid reality
beneath the superficially just and civilized surface of the
society of his time.

The Beggar's Opera is a comedy, of course. The play ends with
Macheath reprieved and at last acknowledging, furtively
enough, that Polly is his wife; the final couplet, 'But think of
this maxim, and put off your sorrow,/The wretch of today,
may be happy tomorrow' (III.xvii), suggests, perhaps rather
tentatively, that misery need not be permanent and that
happiness is possible. But, as the Beggar has only just re-
minded us, this cheerful conclusion is an absurdity tacked on
to gratify the degenerate taste of the town. The earlier conclusion, pronounced by the Beggar in his final speech, is
unacceptable because it expresses a harsh truth about contemporary society, a vision that 'the town' – the fashionable
middle classes of Gay's London – finds too uncomfortable to
contemplate, preferring to retreat instead into the extravagant
play-world of the opera. But the grim vision of cynicism and
rapacity beneath the glitter is insinuated into Gay's comedy
from its opening scene, and it is to the Beggar's first, rejected,
conclusion that *The Beggar's Opera* naturally moves.

The irony, of course, is that 'the town' took to *The Beggar's
Opera* as to no play before it. Moved by a natural wish to
capitalize on its success, Gay composed a sequel, *Polly*, in the

summer of 1728, but the staging of this rather feeble after-crop was forbidden by the authorities. As Lord Hervey wrote in his *Memoirs*: 'Sir Robert Walpole resolved, rather than suffer himself to be produced for thirty nights together upon the stage in the person of a highwayman, to make use of his friend the Duke of Grafton's authority as Lord Chamberlain to put a stop to the representation of it.'[31]

The Beggar's Opera was the last, great, success of Gay's career. The fate of its sequel bore out the play's most cynical assumptions about public life and Gay wrote little more after *Polly* – a couple of minor plays and a second volume of *Fables* complete the catalogue of his works. He lived increasingly away from the intrigues and glamour of the town, spending most of his time at the country house of his last patroness and friend the Duchess of Queensberry. He died, aged forty-seven, in December 1732. The air of surface good-humour masking a wry, even bitter, sense of the pervasiveness of human folly and wickedness which runs through Gay's work at its best and which is displayed most brilliantly in the complex ironies of *The Beggar's Opera* is perfectly reflected in the epitaph he composed for himself:

> Life is a jest; and all things show it,
> I thought so once; but now I know it.[32]

31. *Lord Hervey's Memoirs*, edited by Romney Sedgwick (London, 1952), p. 52.
32. *John Gay: Poetry and Prose*, 1, 253.

RECOMMENDED READING

Other Editions of 'The Beggar's Opera'

John Gay, *Dramatic Works*, edited by John Fuller, 2 vols. (Oxford, 1983). *The Beggar's Opera* is in vol. II, pp. 1–65.

John Gay, *The Beggar's Opera*, edited by Edgar V. Roberts, music edited by Edward Smith, Regents Restoration Drama Series (London, 1969). Prints the music, with keyboard accompaniment.

John Gay, *The Beggar's Opera*, edited by Peter Elfed Lewis (Edinburgh, 1973). Very fully annotated.

Other Works by Gay

John Gay: Poetry and Prose, edited by Vinton A. Dearing with the assistance of Charles E. Beckwith, 2 vols. (Oxford, 1974).

Life and Letters

W. H. Irving, *John Gay: Favorite of the Wits* (Durham, North Carolina, 1940). The standard biography.

The Letters of John Gay, edited by C. F. Burgess (Oxford, 1966).

Other Reading

Bertrand H. Bronson, 'The Beggar's Opera', in *Studies in the Comic*, University of California Publications in English, vol. 8, no. 2 (Berkeley, California, 1941), pp. 197–231 (reprinted in *Restoration Drama: Modern Essays in Criticism*, edited by John Loftis, New York, 1966, pp. 298–327). The best study of operatic parody in *The Beggar's Opera*.

William Empson, *Some Versions of Pastoral* (London, 1935). The chapter on *The Beggar's Opera* provides a fascinating, if contentious, reading of the play.

Michael Denning, 'Beggars and Thieves', *Literature and History*, vol. 8, no. 1 (Spring, 1982), 41–55. A stimulatingly radical reading of *The Beggar's Opera*.

M. Dorothy George, *London Life in the Eighteenth Century* (London, 1951). An indispensable source of social and demographic information.

Gerald Howson, *Thief-Taker General: The Rise and Fall of Jonathan Wild* (London, 1970). The best study of the criminal milieu of Gay's London.

Peter Lewis, *John Gay: The Beggar's Opera* (London, 1976). A readable introduction to the play.

NOTE ON THE MUSIC

The tunes Gay chose for his songs in *The Beggar's Opera* were all in popular currency in 1728. The majority of them – forty-one out of a total of sixty-nine airs – were traditional anonymous broadside ballad tunes, the rest were borrowed from contemporary songwriters and opera composers. The background and history of the broadside ballad tunes Gay used is studied in Claude M. Simpson's comprehensive work *The British Broadside Ballad and Its Music* (New Brunswick, New Jersey, 1966). There is no such satisfactory authority for the other airs; the best account is probably that provided by A. E. H. Swaen, 'The Airs and Tunes of John Gay's *Beggar's Opera*', *Anglia*, 43 (1919), 152–90.

Though there is no doubt that Gay conceived of the songs as an integral part of *The Beggar's Opera*, there is some evidence that he first intended that the Airs should be sung unaccompanied and that he was persuaded that they should be supported by orchestral accompaniments only in the course of rehearsal (see William Eben Schultz, *John Gay's 'Beggar's Opera': Its Content, History and Influence*, New Haven, Connecticut, 1923, pp. 126–7). The accompaniments were arranged by John Christopher Pepusch, an émigré from Berlin who was the music director of the playhouse in Lincoln's Inn Fields where *The Beggar's Opera* was first produced; Pepusch also composed the overture.

The tunes to the airs in Gay's play, with keyboard accompaniments based on Pepusch's originals, are included as Appendix A in the Regents Restoration Drama Series edition of *The Beggar's Opera* edited by Edgar V. Roberts, music edited by Edward Smith (London, 1969). Several gramophone records of the tunes are available.

NOTE ON THE TEXT

The text here reproduced is based on the third, quarto, edition of 1729. Both spelling and, to a certain extent, punctuation have been modernized to accord with current practice.

The facsimile title page opposite is of the 1728 edition. The Latin epigraph ('We know these things to be nothing' – Martial, *Epigrams*, XIII, ii) is a mock-modest disclaimer designed to deflect criticism.

THE
BEGGAR's
OPERA.

As it is Acted at the

THEATRE-ROYAL

IN

LINCOLNS-INN-FIELDS.

Written by Mr. *G A Y.*

——*Nos hæc novimus esse nihil.*   Mart.

To which is Added,

The MUSICK *Engrav'd on* COPPER-PLATES.

L O N D O N:

Printed for JOHN WATTS, at the Printing-Office
in *Wild-Court*, near *Lincoln's-Inn-Fields.*
MDCCXXVIII.
[Price 1*s.* 6*d.*]

DRAMATIS PERSONAE

PEACHUM[1]	underworld 'fence' and thief-taker
Mrs PEACHUM	his common-law wife
POLLY PEACHUM	their daughter
LOCKIT	Newgate[2] jailer in league with Peachum
LUCY LOCKIT	his daughter
MACHEATH[3]	highwayman
BEGGAR	fictional author of the play
PLAYER	
FILCH	member of Peachum's household

JEMMY TWITCHER[4]
CROOK-FINGERED JACK
WAT DREARY
ROBIN OF BAGSHOT[5] } members of Macheath's gang
NIMMING[6] NED
HARRY PADINGTON[7]

1. *Peachum:* i.e. 'peach 'em'. To 'peach' was to impeach or inform against a fellow-criminal; see editors' introduction, pp. 20–21.

2. *Newgate:* from its origins in the twelfth century until it was demolished in 1902, Newgate was the most important and most infamous of London's many prisons; it was located to the north-west of St Paul's, where Newgate Street met the old City wall. The Sessions House, better known as the Old Bailey, where criminal trials were held, was a few yards to the south.

3. *Macheath:* i.e. 'son of the heath'. The heathlands around London were notorious for the frequent highway robberies that took place there; Macheath is a highwayman.

4. *Twitcher:* a pick-pocket.

5. *Bagshot:* Bagshot Heath was a favourite haunt of highwaymen.

6. *Nimming:* stealing.

7. *Padington:* a 'pad' was a highwayman. The gallows at Tyburn were located in the parish of Paddington and a day on which executions took place was known as a 'Paddington Fair day'.

MATT OF THE MINT[8]
BEN BUDGE[9]   } members of Macheath's gang

DIANA TRAPES[10]
Mrs COAXER
DOLLY TRULL[11]
Mrs VIXEN
BETTY DOXY[12]   } women of the Town
JENNY DIVER[13]
Mrs SLAMMEKIN[14]
SUKY TAWDRY
MOLLY BRAZEN

8. *The Mint:* the parish of St George in Southwark. Once a sanctuary for debtors, it became a refuge for outlaws of all kinds; see p. 105, note 35.

9. *Budge:* a burglar specializing in the theft of clothes.

10. *Trapes:* a slatternly woman.

11. *Trull:* a prostitute.

12. *Doxy:* a female beggar, a prostitute.

13. *Diver:* a pick-pocket.

14. *Slammekin:* a slattern or slut.

INTRODUCTION

BEGGAR, PLAYER

BEGGAR: If poverty be a title to poetry, I am sure nobody can dispute mine. I own myself of the Company of Beggars; and I make one at their weekly festivals at St Giles's.[1] I have a small yearly salary for my catches,[2] and am welcome to a dinner there whenever I please, which is more than most poets can say.

PLAYER: As we live by the Muses, 'tis but gratitude in us to encourage poetical merit wherever we find it. The Muses, contrary to all other ladies, pay no distinction to dress, and never partially mistake the pertness of embroidery for wit, nor the modesty of want for dullness. Be the author who he will, we push his play as far as it will go. So (though you are in want) I wish you success heartily.

BEGGAR: This piece I own was originally writ for the celebrating the marriage of James Chanter and Moll Lay,[3] two most excellent ballad singers. I have introduced the similes that are in all your celebrated operas: the swallow, the moth, the bee, the ship, the flower, etc. Besides, I have a prison scene which the ladies always reckon charmingly pathetic. As to the parts, I have observed such a nice impartiality to our two ladies, that it is impossible for either of them to take offence.

1. *St Giles's:* the parish of St Giles's-in-the-Fields, to the east of what is now the Charing Cross Road; a crime-ridden slum in the eighteenth century. Hogarth's print *Gin Lane* (1751) shows a scene in St Giles's.

2. *catches:* 'rounds'; popular songs in which the singers take up the words and melody in sequence.

3. *James Chanter and Moll Lay:* their names reflect their disreputable occupation; ballad singers often operated in league with pick-pockets.

I hope I may be forgiven, that I have not made my opera throughout unnatural, like those in vogue; for I have no recitative: excepting this, as I have consented to have neither prologue nor epilogue, it must be allowed an opera in all its forms. The piece indeed hath been heretofore frequently represented by ourselves in our great room at St Giles's, so that I cannot too often acknowledge your charity in bringing it now on the stage.

PLAYER: But I see 'tis time for us to withdraw; the actors are preparing to begin. Play away the overture.

[*Exeunt.*]

ACT I

SCENE I *Peachum's house*

[PEACHUM *sitting at a table with a large book of accounts before him.*]

AIR 1 An old woman clothed in grey

Through all the employments of life
   Each neighbour abuses his brother;
Whore and rogue they call husband and wife:
   All professions be-rogue one another.
The priest calls the lawyer a cheat,
   The lawyer be-knaves the divine;
And the statesman, because he's so great,
   Thinks his trade as honest as mine.

A lawyer is an honest employment, so is mine. Like me too he acts in a double capacity, both against rogues and for 'em; for 'tis but fitting that we should protect and encourage cheats, since we live by them.

SCENE II

PEACHUM, FILCH

FILCH: Sir, Black Moll hath sent word her trial comes on in the afternoon, and she hopes you will order matters so as to bring her off.[1]

---

1. *Sir . . . bring her off:* Filch's speech stresses at the outset the corruption of the legal system. Peachum, if he wishes, can arrange for Black Moll's acquittal, irrespective of her guilt.

PEACHUM: Why, she may plead her belly[2] at worst; to my knowledge she hath taken care of that security. But as the wench is very active and industrious, you may satisfy her that I'll soften the evidence.

FILCH: Tom Gagg, sir, is found guilty.

PEACHUM: A lazy dog! When I took him the time before, I told him what he would come to if he did not mend his hand. This is death without reprieve. I may venture to book him. [*writes*] For Tom Gagg, forty pounds.[3] Let Betty Sly know that I'll save her from transportation,[4] for I can get more by her staying in England.

FILCH: Betty hath brought more goods into our lock to-year[5] than any five of the gang; and in truth, 'tis a pity to lose so good a customer.[6]

PEACHUM: If none of the gang take her off,[7] she may, in the common course of business, live a twelve-month longer. I love to let women scape. A good sportsman always lets the hen partridges fly, because the breed of the game depends upon them. Besides, here the law allows us no reward; there is nothing to be got by the death of women – except our wives.

FILCH: Without dispute, she is a fine woman! 'Twas to her I was obliged for my education, and (to say a bold word) she hath trained up more young fellows to the business[8] than the gaming-table.

PEACHUM: Truly, Filch, thy observation is right. We and the

---

2. *plead her belly*: a woman could not be executed if she could prove she was pregnant.

3. *forty pounds*: the reward paid by the government to an informer whose evidence led to conviction for theft and the subsequent execution of the criminal.

4. *transportation*: criminals convicted of certain offences could be transported to exile in North America or the West Indies for terms ranging from seven years to life.

5. *lock*: a warehouse where stolen goods were stored; *to-year*: this year.

6. *customer*: anyone with whom one has dealings; not necessarily a purchaser.

7. *take her off*: inform against her.

8. *the business*: i.e. thievery.

surgeons are more beholden to women than all the professions besides.[9]

AIR II The bonny grey-eyed morn

FILCH: *'Tis woman that seduces all mankind,*
          By her we first were taught the wheedling arts:
          Her very eyes can cheat; when most she's kind,
          She tricks us of our money with our hearts.
          For her, like wolves by night we roam for prey,
          And practise ev'ry fraud to bribe her charms;
          For suits of love, like law, are won by pay,
          And beauty must be fee'd into our arms.

PEACHUM: But make haste to Newgate,[10] boy, and let my friends know what I intend; for I love to make them easy one way or other.

FILCH: When a gentleman is long kept in suspense, penitence may break his spirit ever after. Besides, certainty gives a man a good air upon his trial, and makes him risk another without fear or scruple. But I'll away, for 'tis a pleasure to be the messenger of comfort to friends in affliction.

SCENE III

PEACHUM

But 'tis now high time to look about me for a decent execution against next Sessions.[11] I hate a lazy rogue, by whom one can get nothing 'till he is hanged. A register of the

---

9. *We and the surgeons . . . besides:* The expense of maintaining women turns men to crime. The surgeons are 'beholden to women' because of the money they earn by treating venereal disease.

10. *Newgate:* London's principal prison from the twelfth to the nineteenth centuries.

11. *Sessions:* the assizes or criminal trials which were held eight times a year at the Sessions House in the Old Bailey.

gang, [*reading*] Crook-fingered Jack. A year and a half in the service; let me see how much the stock owes to his industry; one, two, three, four, five gold watches, and seven silver ones. A mighty clean-handed fellow! Sixteen snuff-boxes, five of them true gold. Six dozen of handkerchiefs, four silver-hilted swords, half a dozen of shirts, three tye-perriwigs, and a piece of broad cloth.[12] Considering these are only the fruits of his leisure hours, I don't know a prettier[13] fellow, for no man alive hath a more engaging presence of mind upon the road.[14] Wat Dreary, alias Brown Will, an irregular dog, who hath an underhand way of disposing of his goods. I'll try him only for a Sessions or two longer upon his good behaviour. Harry Padington, a poor petty-larceny[15] rascal, without the least genius; that fellow, though he were to live these six months, will never come to the gallows with any credit. Slippery Sam; he goes off the next Sessions, for the villain hath the impudence to have views of following his trade as a tailor, which he calls an honest employment. Mat of the Mint; listed[16] not above a month ago, a promising sturdy fellow, and diligent in his way; somewhat too bold and hasty, and may raise good contributions on the public,[17] if he does not cut himself short by murder. Tom Tipple, a guzzling soaking sot, who is always too drunk to stand himself, or to make others stand. A cart[18] is absolutely necessary for him. Robin of Bagshot,

---

12. *handkerchiefs:* made of lace, linen, or other expensive material, these were valuable items; *tye-perriwigs:* a wig in which the hair was drawn back to form a tail tied with black ribbon at the nape of the neck; *broad cloth:* fine-quality black cloth, used chiefly for men's garments.

13. *prettier:* more skilful.

14. *upon the road:* i.e. Crook-fingered Jack is a highwayman.

15. *petty-larceny:* non-capital theft; see editors' introduction, p. 17.

16. *listed:* enlisted.

17. *good contributions on the public:* i.e. Matt of the Mint will contribute usefully to the prosperity of the gang at the expense of the public whom he robs.

18. *cart:* condemned criminals were taken in a cart to the gallows to be hanged.

alias Gorgon, alias Bluff Bob, alias Carbuncle, alias Bob
Booty.[19]

SCENE IV

PEACHUM, MRS PEACHUM

MRS PEACHUM: What of Bob Booty, husband? I hope nothing
bad hath betided him. You know, my dear, he's a favourite
customer of mine. 'Twas he made me a present of this ring.

PEACHUM: I have set his name down in the Black-List,[20] that's
all, my dear; he spends his life among women,[21] and as soon
as his money is gone, one or other of the ladies will hang him
for the reward, and there's forty pound lost to us forever.

MRS PEACHUM: You know, my dear, I never meddle in
matters of death; I always leave those affairs to you. Women
indeed are bitter bad judges in these cases, for they are so
partial to the brave that they think every man handsome
who is going to the camp or the gallows.

AIR III Cold and raw

> *If any wench Venus's girdle[22] wear,*
> *Though she be never so ugly;*
> *Lilies and roses will quickly appear,*
> *And her face look wond'rous smugly.[23]*

---

19. *Robin of Bagshot . . . Bob Booty:* taken by contemporary audiences to refer to Sir Robert
Walpole – see editors' introduction, pp. 26–7. 'Bluff' meant 'blustering' or 'surly', rather
than implying jovial good humour, as it does now. A carbuncle was a red spot or pimple
caused by habitual drunkenness.

20. *Black-List:* i.e. the list of those gang members whom Peachum has decided to send to
the gallows.

21. *he spends his life among women:* another jibe at Walpole; see editors' introduction,
p. 27.

22. *Venus's girdle:* a belt belonging to Venus, goddess of love, which had the power to
make anyone who wore it instantly desirable.

23. *smugly:* attractive.

> *Beneath the left ear so fit but a cord,*
> *(A rope so charming a zone is!)*
> *The youth in his cart hath the air of a lord,*
> *And we cry, 'There dies an Adonis!'*[24]

But really, husband, you should not be too hard-hearted, for you never had a finer, braver set of men than at present. We have not had a murder among them all, these seven months. And truly, my dear, that is a great blessing.

PEACHUM: What a dickens is the woman always a whimpering about murder for? No gentleman is ever looked upon the worse for killing a man in his own defence; and if business cannot be carried on without it, what would you have a gentleman do?

MRS PEACHUM: If I am in the wrong, my dear, you must excuse me, for nobody can help the frailty of an over-scrupulous conscience.

PEACHUM: Murder is as fashionable a crime as a man can be guilty of. How many fine gentlemen have we in Newgate every year, purely upon that article! If they have wherewithal to persuade the jury to bring it in manslaughter, what are they the worse for it? So, my dear, have done upon this subject. Was Captain[25] Macheath here this morning, for the bank-notes[26] he left with you last week?

MRS PEACHUM: Yes, my dear; and though the bank hath stopped payment, he was so cheerful and so agreeable! Sure there is not a finer gentleman upon the road than the Captain! If he comes from Bagshot[27] at any reasonable hour

24. *Adonis:* a handsome youth, beloved of Venus; hence the type of male beauty.

25. *Captain:* wild young men-about-town frequently awarded themselves this rank; the custom probably derives from the roaring, duelling, swaggering *capitano* in the Italian *commedia dell'arte* tradition.

26. *bank-notes:* receipts for money deposited; these circulated as currency and were made out to the bearer, so a thief could cash them if he got to the bank on which they were drawn before the notice to stop payment arrived.

27. *Bagshot:* a notorious haunt of highwaymen.

he hath promised to make one this evening with Polly and me, and Bob Booty, at a party of quadrille.[28] Pray, my dear, is the Captain rich?

PEACHUM: The Captain keeps too good company ever to grow rich. Marybone[29] and the chocolate-houses[30] are his undoing. The man that proposes to get money by play should have the education of a fine gentleman, and be trained up to it from his youth.

MRS PEACHUM: Really, I am sorry upon Polly's account the Captain hath not more discretion. What business hath he to keep company with lords and gentlemen? He should leave them to prey upon one another.

PEACHUM: Upon Polly's account! What, a plague, does the woman mean? Upon Polly's account!

MRS PEACHUM: Captain Macheath is very fond of the girl.

PEACHUM: And what then?

MRS PEACHUM: If I have any skill in the ways of women, I am sure Polly thinks him a very pretty man.

PEACHUM: And what then? You would not be so mad to have the wench marry him! Gamesters and highwaymen are generally very good to their whores, but they are very devils to their wives.

MRS PEACHUM: But if Polly should be in love, how should we help her, or how can she help herself? Poor girl, I am in the utmost concern about her.

AIR IV Why is your faithful slave disdained?

> *If love the virgin's heart invade,*
> *How, like a moth, the simple maid*
> *Still plays about the flame!*
> *If soon she be not made a wife,*

28. *quadrille:* a fashionable card game.

29. *Marybone:* now Marylebone, in Gay's time the centre of the London gambling world.

30. *chocolate-houses:* fashionable male meeting-places where hot cocoa was served and where gambling took place.

> Her honour's singed, and then for life,
> She's – what I dare not name.

PEACHUM: Look ye, wife. A handsome wench in our way of business is as profitable as at the bar of a Temple[31] coffee-house, who looks upon it as her livelihood to grant every liberty but one. You see I would indulge the girl as far as prudently we can. In anything, but marriage! After that, my dear, how shall we be safe? Are we not then in her husband's power? For a husband hath the absolute power over all a wife's secrets but her own. If the girl had the discretion of a court lady, who can have a dozen young fellows at her ear without complying with one, I should not matter it; but Polly is tinder, and a spark will at once set her on a flame. Married! If the wench does not know her own profit, sure she knows her own pleasure better than to make herself a property![32] My daughter to me should be, like a court lady to a minister of state, a key to the whole gang. Married! If the affair is not already done, I'll terrify her from it, by the example of our neighbours.

MRS PEACHUM: May-hap, my dear, you may injure the girl. She loves to imitate the fine ladies, and she may only allow the Captain liberties in the view of interest.

PEACHUM: But 'tis your duty, my dear, to warn the girl against her ruin, and to instruct her how to make the most of her beauty. I'll go to her this moment, and sift her. In the meantime, wife, rip out the coronets and marks of these dozen of cambric handkerchiefs, for I can dispose of them this afternoon to a chap in the City.[33]

---

31. *Temple:* one of the London Inns of Court, where lawyers are trained and practise.

32. *make herself a property:* when a woman married, her possessions legally became her husband's.

33. *coronets and marks:* means of identification embroidered on garments; coronets identify the owner as a member of the peerage; *cambric:* very fine-quality linen; *chap:* short for 'chapman', a dealer.

SCENE V

MRS PEACHUM

Never was a man more out of the way in an argument than my husband! Why must our Polly, forsooth, differ from her sex, and love only her husband? And why must Polly's marriage, contrary to all observation, make her the less followed by other men? All men are thieves in love, and like a woman the better for being another's property.

AIR V *Of all the simple things we do*

A maid is like the golden ore,
Which hath guineas intrinsical in't,
Whose worth is never known, before
It is tried[34] and impressed in the Mint.
A wife's like a guinea in gold,
Stamped with the name of her spouse;
Now here, now there; is bought, or is sold;
And is current in every house.

SCENE VI

MRS PEACHUM, FILCH

MRS PEACHUM: Come hither Filch. I am as fond of this child, as though my mind misgave me he were my own. He hath as fine a hand at picking a pocket as a woman, and is as nimble-fingered as a juggler. If an unlucky Session does not cut the rope of thy life, I pronounce, boy, thou wilt be a great man in history. Where was your post last night, my boy?

FILCH: I plied at the opera, madam; and considering 'twas

34. *tried:* refined, purified.

neither dark nor rainy, so that there was no great hurry in getting chairs and coaches, made a tolerable hand on't.[35] These seven handkerchiefs, madam.

MRS PEACHUM: Coloured ones, I see. They are of sure sale from our warehouse at Redriff[36] among the seamen.

FILCH: And this snuff-box.

MRS PEACHUM: Set in gold! A pretty encouragement this to a young beginner.

FILCH: I had a fair tug at a charming gold watch. Pox take the tailors for making the fobs[37] so deep and narrow! It stuck by the way, and I was forced to make my escape under a coach. Really, madam, I fear I shall be cut off in the flower of my youth, so that every now and then (since I was pumped[38]) I have thoughts of taking up[39] and going to sea.

MRS PEACHUM: You should go to Hockley in the Hole,[40] and to Marybone, child, to learn valour. These are the schools that have bred so many brave men. I thought, boy, by this time, thou hadst lost fear as well as shame. Poor lad! How little does he know as yet of the Old Bailey![41] For the first fact I'll insure thee from being hanged; and going to sea, Filch, will come time enough upon a sentence of transportation. But now, since you have nothing better to do, even go to your book, and learn your catechism;[42] for really a man

35. *considering . . . hand on't:* had it been dark or wet, the patrons coming out of the Opera House would have been hurrying to their coaches and sedan chairs, giving Filch safer opportunities to pick their pockets.

36. *Redriff:* Rotherhithe, in London's dockland.

37. *fobs:* pockets in the front of the breeches.

38. *pumped:* pick-pockets caught in the act were frequently held under a water pump.

39. *taking up:* enlisting as a sailor.

40. *Hockley in the Hole:* near Clerkenwell, the scene of bear and bull-baiting, cockfights, wrestling, and other rough sports.

41. *the Old Bailey:* London's criminal court, where the Sessions were held. It was located just to the south of Newgate Prison.

42. *go . . . catechism:* first offenders convicted of certain felonies could have their sentences reduced from death to transportation, a fine, or a whipping if they could plead 'benefit of clergy', which meant being able to show that they were literate; the test was to read a brief passage from the scriptures, usually the first verse of Psalm 51, which became

makes but an ill figure in the Ordinary's paper,[43] who cannot give a satisfactory answer to his questions. But, hark you, my lad. Don't tell me a lie; for you know I hate a liar. Do you know of anything that hath passed between Captain Macheath and our Polly?

FILCH: I beg you, madam, don't ask me; for I must either tell a lie to you or to Miss Polly; for I promised her I would not tell.

MRS PEACHUM: But when the honour of our family is concerned –

FILCH: I shall lead a sad life with Miss Polly, if ever she come to know that I told you. Besides, I would not willingly forfeit my own honour by betraying anybody.

MRS PEACHUM: Yonder comes my husband and Polly. Come, Filch, you shall go with me into my own room, and tell me the whole story. I'll give thee a glass of a most delicious cordial[44] that I keep for my own drinking.

SCENE VII

PEACHUM, POLLY

POLLY: I know as well as any of the fine ladies how to make the most of myself and of my man too. A woman knows how to be mercenary, though she hath never been in a court or at an assembly.[45] We have it in our natures, papa. If I allow

---

known as the 'neck verse'. This custom was a relic of the Middle Ages, when clerics were tried by Ecclesiastical Courts and could escape with lighter sentences for certain crimes for which laymen were punished by death; the original assumption was that only clerics were likely to be literate.

43. *Ordinary's paper*: the Ordinary was the Chaplain of Newgate; one of his duties was to administer the literacy test to felons pleading benefit of clergy. Sensational accounts of the dying confessions and repentance of condemned criminals supposedly reported by the Ordinary were commonly published, and Mrs Peachum may be thinking of these.

44. *cordial*: a strong, sweet, alcoholic beverage.

45. *assembly*: a fashionable gathering, normally including music and dancing, and featuring flirtation and the exchange of gossip.

Captain Macheath some trifling liberties, I have this watch and other visible marks of his favour to show for it. A girl who cannot grant some things, and refuse what is most material, will make but a poor hand of her beauty, and soon be thrown upon the common.[46]

AIR VI   What shall I do to show how much I love her

> Virgins are like the fair flower in its lustre,
>   Which in the garden enamels the ground;
> Near it the bees in play flutter and cluster,
>   And gaudy butterflies frolic around.
> But, when once plucked, 'tis no longer alluring,
>   To Covent Garden[47] 'tis sent (as yet sweet),
> There fades, and shrinks, and grows past all enduring,
>   Rots, stinks, and dies, and is trod under feet.

PEACHUM: You know, Polly, I am not against your toying and trifling with a customer in the way of business, or to get out a secret, or so. But if I find out that you have played the fool and are married, you jade you, I'll cut your throat, hussy. Now you know my mind.

SCENE VIII

PEACHUM, POLLY, MRS PEACHUM

AIR VII   Oh London is a fine town

MRS PEACHUM, *in a very great passion.*

> Our Polly is a sad slut! nor heeds what we have taught her.
> I wonder any man alive will ever rear a daughter!

46. *common*: a complex pun: the girl will be turned out onto common-land, will become 'common' – i.e. a prostitute – and will be condemned as such by the common law.

47. *Covent Garden:* London's most important flower and vegetable market, but also the district most notorious for prostitution.

For she must have both hoods and gowns, and hoops[48] *to swell her*
    pride,
With scarfs and stays,[49] *and gloves and lace; and she will have*
    men beside;
And when she's dressed with care and cost, all-tempting, fine and
    gay,
As men should serve a cowcumber,[50] *she flings herself away.*
    Our Polly is a sad slut, etc.

You baggage! You hussy! You inconsiderate jade! Had you
been hanged, it would not have vexed me, for that might
have been your misfortune; but to do such a mad thing by
choice! The wench is married, husband.

PEACHUM: Married! The Captain is a bold man, and will risk
anything for money; to be sure he believes her a fortune. Do
you think your mother and I should have lived comfortably
so long together, if ever we had been married? Baggage!

MRS PEACHUM: I knew she was always a proud slut; and now
the wench hath played the fool and married, because forsooth she would do like the gentry. Can you support the
expense of a husband, hussy, in gaming, drinking and
whoring? Have you money enough to carry on the daily
quarrels of man and wife about who shall squander most?
There are not many husbands and wives, who can bear the
charges of plaguing one another in a handsome way. If you
must be married, could you introduce nobody into our
family but a highwayman? Why, thou foolish jade, thou wilt
be as ill-used, and as much neglected, as if thou hadst
married a lord!

PEACHUM: Let not your anger, my dear, break through the
rules of decency, for the Captain looks upon himself in the

---

48. *hoops:* the circular (hooped) petticoats fashionable at the time. Addison makes fun of
them in a famous *Spectator* essay (no. 127).

49. *stays:* corsets.

50. *cowcumber:* cucumber; regarded at the time as not worth the trouble it took to prepare
them.

military capacity, as a gentleman by his profession. Besides what he hath already, I know he is in a fair way of getting,[51] or of dying; and both these ways, let me tell you, are most excellent chances for a wife. Tell me hussy, are you ruined or no?[52]

MRS PEACHUM: With Polly's fortune, she might very well have gone off to a person of distinction. Yes, that you might, you pouting slut!

PEACHUM: What, is the wench dumb? Speak, or I'll make you plead by squeezing out an answer from you.[53] Are you really bound wife to him, or are you only upon liking?[54] [*Pinches her.*]

POLLY: Oh! [*Screaming.*]

MRS PEACHUM: How the mother is to be pitied who hath handsome daughters! Locks, bolts, bars, and lectures of morality are nothing to them: they break through them all. They have as much pleasure in cheating a father and mother, as in cheating at cards.

PEACHUM: Why, Polly, I shall soon know if you are married, by Macheath's keeping from our house.

AIR VIII Grim King of the ghosts

POLLY: *Can love be controlled by advice?*
              Will Cupid our mothers obey?
              Though my heart were as frozen as ice,
              At his flame 'twould have melted away.

51. *getting:* becoming rich.

52. *are . . . no?:* 'ruined' in this context normally referred to a girl's having lost her virginity before marriage – Peachum means exactly the opposite. This is an excellent example of the play's characteristic cynicism about marriage; see editors' introduction, p. 28.

53. *Speak . . . you:* prisoners who refused to plead either guilty or not guilty were forced to do so by having heavy weights placed on their chests; if they remained stubborn, they were pressed to death.

54. *upon liking:* on approval or trial.

> When he kissed me so closely he pressed,
>   'Twas so sweet that I must have complied:
> So I thought it both safest and best
>   To marry, for fear you should chide.

MRS PEACHUM: Then all the hopes of our family are gone for ever and ever!

PEACHUM: And Macheath may hang his father and mother-in-law, in hope to get into their daughter's fortune.[55]

POLLY: I did not marry him (as 'tis the fashion) coolly and deliberately for honour or money. But, I love him.

MRS PEACHUM: Love him! Worse and worse! I thought the girl had been better bred. O husband, husband! Her folly makes me mad! My head swims! I'm distracted! I can't support myself – O! [*Faints.*]

PEACHUM: See, wench, to what a condition you have reduced your poor mother! A glass of cordial, this instant. How the poor woman takes it to heart! [POLLY *goes out, and returns with it.*] Ah hussy, now this is the only comfort your mother has left!

POLLY: Give her another glass, sir; my mama drinks double the quantity whenever she is out of order. This, you see, fetches her.

MRS PEACHUM: The girl shows such a readiness, and so much concern, that I could almost find in my heart to forgive her.

AIR IX O Jenny, O Jenny, where hast thou been

MRS PEACHUM:
>   O Polly, you might have toyed and kissed.
>   By keeping men off, you keep them on.

POLLY:
>   But he so teased me,
>   And he so pleased me,
>   What I did, you must have done.

---

55. *And Macheath . . . fortune:* Macheath has the power to inform on Mr and Mrs Peachum as receivers of stolen goods, and so inherit the wealth they leave to Polly.

MRS PEACHUM: Not with a highwayman – you sorry slut!

PEACHUM: A word with you, wife. 'Tis no new thing for a wench to take man without consent of parents. You know 'tis the frailty of woman, my dear.

MRS PEACHUM: Yes, indeed, the sex is frail. But the first time a woman is frail, she should be somewhat nice[56] methinks, for then or never is the time to make her fortune. After that, she hath nothing to do but to guard herself from being found out, and she may do what she pleases.

PEACHUM: Make yourself a little easy; I have a thought shall soon set all matters again to rights. Why so melancholy, Polly? Since what is done cannot be undone, we must all endeavour to make the best of it.

MRS PEACHUM: Well, Polly; as far as one woman can forgive another, I forgive thee. Your father is too fond of you, hussy.

POLLY: Then all my sorrows are at an end.

MRS PEACHUM: A mighty likely speech in troth, for a wench who is just married!

AIR X Thomas, I cannot

POLLY: *I, like a ship in storms, was tossed;*
           Yet afraid to put in to land;
           For seized in the port the vessel's lost,
           Whose treasure is contreband.
               The waves are laid,
               My duty's paid.
           O joy beyond expression!
               Thus, safe ashore,
               I ask no more,
           My all is in my possession.

PEACHUM: I hear customers in t'other room. Go, talk with 'em, Polly; but come to us again, as soon as they are gone. But, heark ye, child, if 'tis the gentleman who was here

56. *nice:* particular.

yesterday about the repeating-watch,[57] say, you believe we can't get intelligence of it, till tomorrow, for I lent it to Suky Straddle, to make a figure with it tonight at a tavern in Drury Lane.[58] If t'other gentleman calls for the silver-hilted sword, you know beetle-browed Jemmy hath it on, and he doth not come from Tunbridge till Tuesday night, so that it cannot be had till then.

SCENE IX

PEACHUM, MRS PEACHUM

PEACHUM: Dear wife, be a little pacified. Don't let your passion run away with your senses. Polly, I grant you, hath done a rash thing.

MRS PEACHUM: If she had had only an intrigue[59] with the fellow, why the very best families have excused and huddled up a frailty of that sort. 'Tis marriage, husband, that makes it a blemish.

PEACHUM: But money, wife, is the true fuller's earth[60] for reputations, there is not a spot or a stain but what it can take out. A rich rogue now-a-days is fit company for any gentleman; and the world, my dear, hath not such a contempt for roguery as you imagine. I tell you, wife, I can make this match turn to our advantage.

MRS PEACHUM: I am very sensible,[61] husband, that Captain Macheath is worth money, but I am in doubt whether he hath not two or three wives already, and then if he should die in a Session or two, Polly's dower would come into dispute.

57. *repeating-watch:* a watch that struck the most recent hour and quarter when a lever was pressed.

58. *Drury Lane:* near Covent Garden; notorious as a haunt for prostitutes.

59. *an intrigue:* a love affair.

60. *fuller's earth:* a type of clay used in cleaning fabrics.

61. *sensible:* aware.

PEACHUM: That, indeed, is a point which ought to be considered.

AIR XI A soldier and a sailor

A fox may steal your hens, sir,
A whore your health and pence, sir,
Your daughter rob your chest, sir,
Your wife may steal your rest, sir,
  A thief your goods and plate.
But this is all but picking,
With rest, pence, chest and chicken;
It ever was decreed, sir,
If lawyer's hand is fee'd, sir,
  He steals your whole estate.

The lawyers are bitter enemies to those in our way. They don't care that anybody should get a clandestine livelihood but themselves.

SCENE X

MRS PEACHUM, PEACHUM, POLLY

POLLY: 'Twas only Nimming Ned. He brought in a damask[62] window curtain, a hoop-petticoat, a pair of silver candlesticks, a perriwig, and one silk stocking, from the fire that happened last night.

PEACHUM: There is not a fellow that is cleverer in his way, and saves more goods out of the fire than Ned. But now, Polly, to your affair; for matters must not be left as they are. You are married then, it seems?

POLLY: Yes, sir.

PEACHUM: And how do you propose to live, child?

---

62. *damask*: a patterned fabric of silk or linen.

POLLY: Like other women, sir, upon the industry of my husband.

MRS PEACHUM: What, is the wench turned fool? A highwayman's wife, like a soldier's, hath as little of his pay, as of his company.

PEACHUM: And had not you the common views of a gentlewoman in your marriage, Polly?

POLLY: I don't know what you mean, sir.

PEACHUM: Of a jointure,[63] and of being a widow.

POLLY: But I love him, sir: how then could I have thoughts of parting with him?

PEACHUM: Parting with him! Why, that is the whole scheme and intention of all marriage articles. The comfortable estate of widowhood, is the only hope that keeps up a wife's spirits. Where is the woman who would scruple to be a wife, if she had it in her power to be a widow whenever she pleased? If you have any views of this sort, Polly, I shall think the match not so very unreasonable.

POLLY: How I dread to hear your advice! Yet I must beg you to explain yourself.

PEACHUM: Secure what he hath got, have him peached[64] the next Sessions, and then at once you are made a rich widow.

POLLY: What, murder the man I love! The blood runs cold at my heart with the very thought of it.

PEACHUM: Fie, Polly! What hath murder to do in the affair? Since the thing sooner or later must happen, I dare say, the Captain himself would like that we should get the reward for his death sooner than a stranger. Why, Polly, the Captain knows, that as 'tis his employment to rob, so 'tis ours to take robbers; every man in his business. So that there is no malice in the case.

MRS PEACHUM: Ay, husband, now you have nicked the

63. *jointure*: a legal arrangement by which husband and wife held their property jointly.
64. *peached*: informed against.

matter.[65] To have him peached is the only thing could ever make me forgive her.

AIR XII Now ponder well, ye parents dear

POLLY: *O, ponder well! be not severe;*
So save a wretched wife!
For on the rope that hangs my dear
Depends poor Polly's life.

MRS PEACHUM: But your duty to your parents, hussy, obliges you to hang him. What would many a wife give for such an opportunity!

POLLY: What is a jointure, what is widowhood to me? I know my heart. I cannot survive him.

AIR XIII Le printemps rappelle aux armes

The turtle[66] thus with plaintive crying,
Her lover dying,
The turtle thus with plaintive crying,
Laments her dove.
Down she drops quite spent with sighing,
Paired in death, as paired in love.

Thus, sir, it will happen to your poor Polly.

MRS PEACHUM: What, is the fool in love in earnest then? I hate thee for being particular:[67] why, wench, thou art a shame to thy very sex.

POLLY: But hear me, mother – if you ever loved –

MRS PEACHUM: Those cursed play-books she reads have been her ruin. One word more, hussy, and I shall knock your brains out, if you have any.

---

65. *nicked the matter:* hit the mark.
66. *turtle:* turtle-dove.
67. *being particular:* either (a) confining yourself to one person, or (b) behaving oddly.

PEACHUM: Keep out of the way, Polly, for fear of mischief, and consider of what is proposed to you.

MRS PEACHUM: Away, hussy. Hang your husband, and be dutiful.

SCENE XI

MRS PEACHUM, PEACHUM

[POLLY *listening.*]

MRS PEACHUM: The thing, husband, must and shall be done. For the sake of intelligence[68] we must take other measures, and have him peached the next Session without her consent. If she will not know her duty, we know ours.

PEACHUM: But really, my dear, it grieves one's heart to take off a great man. When I consider his personal bravery, his fine stratagem,[69] how much we have already got by him, and how much more we may get, methinks I can't find in my heart to have a hand in his death. I wish you could have made Polly undertake it.

MRS PEACHUM: But in a case of necessity – our own lives are in danger.

PEACHUM: Then, indeed, we must comply with the customs of the world, and make gratitude give way to interest. He shall be taken off.

MRS PEACHUM: I'll undertake to manage Polly.

PEACHUM: And I'll prepare matters for the Old Bailey.

68. *For the sake of intelligence:* i.e. because of the incriminating information Macheath possesses; 'because of what he knows about us'.

69. *stratagem:* cunning.

SCENE XII

POLLY

Now I'm a wretch, indeed. Methinks I see him already in the cart, sweeter and more lovely than the nosegay[70] in his hand! I hear the crowd extolling his resolution and intrepidity! What vollies of sighs are sent from the windows of Holborn,[71] that so comely a youth should be brought to disgrace! I see him at the tree![72] The whole circle are in tears! Even butchers weep! Jack Ketch[73] himself hesitates to perform his duty, and would be glad to lose his fee, by a reprieve. What then will become of Polly! As yet I may inform him of their design, and aid him in his escape. It shall be so. But then he flies, absents himself, and I bar my self from his dear dear conversation![74] That too will distract me. If he keep out of the way, my papa and mama may in time relent, and we may be happy. If he stays, he is hanged, and then he is lost forever! He intended to lie concealed in my room, 'till the dusk of the evening: if they are abroad, I'll this instant let him out, lest some accident should prevent him.

[Exit, and returns.]

70. *nosegay:* a small bunch of flowers; nosegays were thrown to condemned criminals as they rode to the gallows.

71. *Holborn:* the route from Newgate to the gallows at Tyburn led down Holborn.

72. *the tree:* the gallows.

73. *Jack Ketch:* generic name for the executioner; the original Jack Ketch was hangman from 1663 to 1686.

74. *conversation:* company; the word also implied sexual intimacy.

SCENE XIII

POLLY, MACHEATH

AIR XIV Pretty parrot, say

MACHEATH: *Pretty Polly, say,*
                  When I was away,
             Did your fancy never stray
                To some newer lover?
POLLY: *Without disguise,*
                   Heaving sighs,
                   Doating eyes,
            My constant heart discover.
              Fondly let me loll!
MACHEATH: *O pretty, pretty Poll.*

POLLY: And are *you* as fond as ever, my dear?

MACHEATH: Suspect my honour, my courage, suspect anything but my love. May my pistols misfire, and my mare slip
her shoulder while I am pursued, if I ever forsake thee!

POLLY: Nay, my dear, I have no reason to doubt you, for I find
in the romance you lent me, none of the great heroes were
ever false in love.

AIR XV Pray, fair one, be kind

MACHEATH: *My heart was so free,*
                 It roved like the bee,
            'Till Polly my passion requited;
                 I sipped each flower,
                 I changed ev'ry hour,
           But here ev'ry flower is united.

POLLY: Were you sentenced to transportation, sure, my dear,
you could not leave me behind you – could you?

MACHEATH: Is there any power, any force that could tear me

from thee? You might sooner tear a pension[75] out of the hands of a courtier, a fee from a lawyer, a pretty woman from a looking-glass, or any woman from Quadrille. But to tear me from thee is impossible!

AIR XVI Over the hills and far away

MACHEATH:	*Were I laid on Greenland's coast,*
	And in my arms embraced my lass;
	Warm amidst eternal frost,
	Too soon the half year's night would pass.
POLLY:	*Were I sold on Indian soil,*
	Soon as the burning day was closed,
	I could mock the sultry toil,
	When on my charmer's breast reposed.
MACHEATH:	*And I would love you all the day,*
POLLY:	*Every night would kiss and play,*
MACHEATH:	*If with me you'd fondly stray*
POLLY:	*Over the hills and far away.*

Yes, I would go with thee. But o! How shall I speak it? I must be torn from thee. We must part.

MACHEATH: How! Part!

POLLY: We must, we must. My papa and mama are set against thy life. They now, even now are in search after thee. They are preparing evidence against thee. Thy life depends upon a moment.

AIR XVII Gin thou wert mine awn thing

O what pain it is to part!
Can I leave thee, can I leave thee?
O what pain it is to part!

75. *pension:* in this context, money paid to a courtier as a reward for assiduous toadying. In his great *Dictionary* published in 1755, Dr Johnson wrote of the word 'pension' that 'in England it is generally understood to mean pay given to a state hireling for treason to his country'.

Can thy Polly ever leave thee?
But lest death my love should thwart,
And bring thee to the fatal cart,
Thus I tear thee from my bleeding heart!
    Fly hence, and let me leave thee.

One kiss and then – one kiss – begone – farewell.

MACHEATH: My hand, my heart, my dear, is so riveted to thine, that I cannot unloose my hold.

POLLY: But my papa may intercept thee, and then I should lose the very glimmering of hope. A few weeks, perhaps, may reconcile us all. Shall thy Polly hear from thee?

MACHEATH: Must I then go?

POLLY: And will not absence change your love?

MACHEATH: If you doubt it, let me stay – and be hanged.

POLLY: O how I fear! How I tremble! Go – But when safety will give you leave, you will be sure to see me again; for 'till then Polly is wretched.

AIR XVIII O the broom

[*Parting, and looking back at each other with fondness; he at one door, she at the other.*]

MACHEATH: *The miser thus a shilling sees,*
        Which he's obliged to pay,
    With sighs resigns it by degrees,
        And fears 'tis gone for aye.

POLLY: *The boy, thus, when his sparrow's flown,*
        The bird in silence eyes;
    But soon as out of sight 'tis gone,
        Whines, whimpers, sobs and cries.

ACT II

SCENE I *A tavern near Newgate*

**JEMMY TWITCHER, CROOK-FINGERED JACK, WAT
DREARY, ROBIN OF BAGSHOT, NIMMING NED, HENRY
PADINGTON, MATT OF THE MINT, BEN BUDGE,** *and the rest
of the gang, at the table, with wine, brandy and tobacco*

BEN BUDGE: But pr'ythee, Matt, what is become of thy brother
Tom? I have not seen him since my return from transportation.

MATT OF THE MINT: Poor brother Tom had an accident this
time twelve-month, and so clever a made fellow[1] he was,
that I could not save him from those flaying rascals the
surgeons; and now, poor man, he is among the otamies at
Surgeon's Hall.[2]

BEN BUDGE: So it seems, his time was come.

JEMMY TWITCHER: But the present time is ours, and nobody
alive hath more. Why are the laws levelled at us? Are we
more dishonest than the rest of mankind? What we win,
gentlemen, is our own by the law of arms, and the right of
conquest.

CROOK-FINGERED JACK: Where shall we find such another
set of practical philosophers, who to a man are above the fear
of death?

WAT DREARY: Sound men, and true!

---

1. *so clever a made fellow:* so well-made a fellow.
2. *those flaying rascals . . . Surgeon's Hall:* surgeons used the bodies of executed criminals
for dissection in anatomy demonstrations; Tom's 'accident' has been to be hanged;
otamies: skeletons.

ROBIN OF BAGSHOT: Of tried courage, and indefatigable industry!

NIMMING NED: Who is there here that would not die for his friend?[3]

HARRY PADINGTON: Who is there here that would betray him for his interest?

MATT OF THE MINT: Show me a gang of courtiers that can say as much.

BEN BUDGE: We are for a just partition of the world, for every man hath a right to enjoy life.

MATT OF THE MINT: We retrench[4] the superfluities of mankind. The world is avaricious, and I hate avarice. A covetous fellow, like a jackdaw,[5] steals what he was never made to enjoy, for the sake of hiding it. These are the robbers of mankind, for money was made for the free-hearted and generous, and where is the injury of taking from another, what he hath not the heart to make use of?

JEMMY TWITCHER: Our several stations for the day are fixed. Good luck attend us all. Fill the glasses.

AIR XIX Fill ev'ry glass

MATT OF THE MINT:
> *Fill every glass, for wine inspires us,*
> > *And fires us*
> > *With courage, love and joy.*
> > *Women and wine should life employ.*
> > *Is there ought else on earth desirous?*

CHORUS: *Fill every glass, etc.*

---

3. *Who is there . . . for his friend?:* Jemmy Twitcher, for one; see III.xiv.

4. *retrench:* cut down, reduce.

5. *jackdaw:* a rook-like bird (*Corvus monedula*), traditionally prone to stealing.

SCENE II

To them enter MACHEATH

MACHEATH: Gentlemen, well met. My heart hath been with you this hour; but an unexpected affair hath detained me. No ceremony, I beg you.

MATT OF THE MINT: We were just breaking up to go upon duty. Am I to have the honour of taking the air with you, sir, this evening upon the heath?[6] I drink a dram now and then with the stage-coachmen in the way of friendship and intelligence; and I know that about this time there will be passengers upon the Western Road, who are worth speaking with.

MACHEATH: I was to have been of that party – but –

MATT OF THE MINT: But what, sir?

MACHEATH: Is there any man who suspects my courage?

MATT OF THE MINT: We have all been witnesses of it.

MACHEATH: My honour and truth to the gang?

MATT OF THE MINT: I'll be answerable for it.

MACHEATH: In the division of our booty, have I ever shown the least marks of avarice or injustice?

MATT OF THE MINT: By these questions something seems to have ruffled you. Are any of us suspected?

MACHEATH: I have a fixed confidence, gentlemen, in you all, as men of honour, and as such I value and respect you. Peachum is a man that is useful to us.

MATT OF THE MINT: Is he about to play us any foul play? I'll shoot him through the head.

MACHEATH: I beg you, gentlemen, act with conduct and discretion. A pistol is your last resort.

MATT OF THE MINT: He knows nothing of this meeting.

MACHEATH: Business cannot go on without him. He is a man who knows the world, and is a necessary agent to us. We

6. *taking . . . heath:* a euphemism for a highway-robbery expedition.

have had a slight difference, and till it is accommodated I
shall be obliged to keep out of his way. Any private dispute
of mine shall be of no ill consequence to my friends. You
must continue to act under his direction, for the moment we
break loose from him, our gang is ruined.

MATT OF THE MINT: As a bawd[7] to a whore, I grant you, he is
to us of great convenience.

MACHEATH: Make him believe I have quitted the gang, which
I can never do but with life. At our private quarters I will
continue to meet you. A week or so will probably reconcile
us.

MATT OF THE MINT: Your instructions shall be observed. 'Tis
now high time for us to repair to our several duties; so till the
evening at our quarters in Moor-fields[8] we bid you farewell.

MACHEATH: I shall wish my self with you. Success attend
you. [*Sits down melancholy at the table.*]

AIR XX March in *Rinaldo*,[9] with drums and trumpets

MATT OF THE MINT:

> *Let us take the road.*
> > *Hark! I hear the sound of coaches!*
> > *The hour of attack approaches,*
> *To your arms, brave boys, and load.*
> > *See the ball I hold!*
> > *Let the chemists toil like asses,*
> > *Our fire their fire surpasses,*
> > *And turns all our lead to gold.*[10]

7. *bawd:* a brothel-keeper or procuress.

8. *Moor-fields:* a disreputable district north of the City, frequented by members of the
underworld.

9. *Rinaldo:* Handel's first English opera (1711). Gay and Handel had been friendly at
least since 1719, when Handel composed his first setting of Gay's masque *Acis and Galatea*.

10. *See the ball . . . to gold:* the highwayman, unlike alchemists ('chemists'), successfully
turns lead into gold; his lead bullet ('ball') and the threat of fire from his pistols enables
him to extract gold from the pockets of his victims.

[*The gang, ranged in the front of the stage, load their pistols, and stick them under their girdles;*[11] *then go off singing the first part in chorus.*]

SCENE III

MACHEATH

What a fool is a fond wench! Polly is most confoundedly bit. I love the sex. And a man who loves money, might as well be contented with one guinea, as I with one woman. The town perhaps hath been as much obliged to me, for recruiting it with free-hearted ladies,[12] as to any recruiting officer in the army. If it were not for us and the other gentlemen of the sword, Drury Lane[13] would be uninhabited.

AIR XXI Would you have a young virgin

> *If the heart of a man is depressed with cares,*
> *The mist is dispelled when a woman appears;*
> *Like the notes of a fiddle, she sweetly, sweetly*
> *Raises the spirits, and charms our ears,*
>> *Roses and lilies her cheeks disclose,*
>> *But her ripe lips are more sweet than those.*
>>> *Press her,*
>>> *Caress her*
>>> *With blisses,*
>>> *Her kisses*
> *Dissolve us in pleasure, and soft repose.*

I must have women. There is nothing unbends the mind like them. Money is not so strong a cordial for the time.[14]

11. *girdles:* belts.

12. *free-hearted ladies:* whores. Macheath's point is that highwaymen and soldiers customarily seduce girls and then abandon them, leaving them no alternative but to take up prostitution.

13. *Drury Lane:* notorious for the number of its prostitutes.

14. *so . . . time:* so invigorating a stimulant for passing the time.

Drawer! [*Enter* DRAWER.] Is the porter gone for all the ladies, according to my directions?

DRAWER: I expect him back every minute. But you know, sir, you sent him as far as Hockley in the Hole, for three of the ladies, for one in Vinegar Yard, and for the rest of them somewhere about Lewkner's Lane.[15] Sure some of them are below, for I hear the bar bell. As they come I will show them up. Coming, coming.

SCENE IV

MACHEATH, MRS COAXER, DOLLY TRULL, MRS VIXEN, BETTY DOXY, JENNY DIVER, MRS SLAMMEKIN, SUKY TAWDRY, and MOLLY BRAZEN

MACHEATH: Dear Mrs Coaxer, you are welcome. You look charmingly today. I hope you don't want the repairs of quality,[16] and lay on paint.[17] Dolly Trull! Kiss me, you slut; are you as amorous as ever, hussy? You are always so taken up with stealing hearts, that you don't allow yourself time to steal anything else. Ah Dolly, thou wilt ever be a coquette! Mrs Vixen, I'm yours, I always loved a woman of wit and spirit; they make charming mistresses, but plaguey wives. Betty Doxy! Come hither, hussy. Do you drink as hard as ever? You had better stick to good wholesome beer; for in troth, Betty, strong-waters will in time ruin your constitution.[18] You should leave those to your betters. What! and my pretty Jenny Diver too! As prim and demure as ever! There is not any prude, though ever so high bred,

15. *Vinegar Yard . . . Lewkner's Lane:* places near Drury Lane and therefore associated with prostitution. Jonathan Wild ran a brothel in Lewkner's Lane in 1713.

16. *quality:* i.e. women of quality; well-born ladies.

17. *paint:* cosmetics.

18. *You had better . . . constitution:* the idea that beer was healthy and sustaining while spirits ('strong-waters') promoted corruption and disease was a commonplace; it is the theme of Hogarth's famous companion prints *Beer Street* and *Gin Lane* (1751).

hath a more sanctified look, with a more mischievous heart. Ah! Thou art a dear artful hypocrite. Mrs Slammekin! As careless and genteel as ever! All you fine ladies, who know your own beauty, affect an undress.[19] But see, here's Suky Tawdry come to contradict what I was saying. Everything she gets one way she lays out upon her back.[20] Why, Suky, you must keep at least a dozen tallymen.[21] Molly Brazen! [*She kisses him.*] That's well done. I love a free-hearted wench. Thou hast a most agreeable assurance, girl, and art as willing as a turtle.[22] But hark! I hear music. The harper is at the door. 'If music be the food of love, play on'.[23] E'er you seat yourselves, ladies, what think you of a dance? Come in. [*Enter* HARPER.] Play the French tune, that Mrs Slammekin was so fond of.

> [*A dance a la ronde in the French manner,*[24]
> *near the end of it this song and chorus.*]

AIR XXII Cotillon

MACHEATH: *Youth's the season made for joys,*
            Love is then our duty,
        She alone who that employs,
        Well deserves her beauty.
            Let's be gay,
            While we may,
        Beauty's a flower, despised in decay.

CHORUS: *Youth's the season etc.*

19. *an undress:* an unformal way of dressing, a 'dishabille'; Macheath is being ironic – Mrs Slammekin, as her name informs us, is a slut.

20. *Everything . . . back:* everything she earns by prostitution she spends on clothes; a bawdy pun.

21. *tallymen:* tradesmen who sold or hired-out clothes to prostitutes; this is the trade followed by Mrs Trapes (III.v).

22. *turtle:* turtle-dove, traditionally associated with amorousness.

23. *'If music . . . play on':* the opening line of Shakespeare's comedy *Twelfth Night.*

24. *A dance a la ronde in the French manner:* a dignified and formal dance; since the dancers are Macheath and the whores, the effect is burlesque.

MACHEATH: *Let us drink and sport today,*
    Ours is not tomorrow.
  Love with youth flies swift away,
    Age is nought but sorrow.
      Dance and sing,
      Time's on the wing,
    Life never knows the return of spring.

CHORUS: *Let us drink etc.*

MACHEATH: Now, pray ladies, take your places. Here fellow. [*Pays the* HARPER.] Bid the drawer bring us more wine. [*Exit* HARPER.] If any of the ladies choose gin, I hope they will be so free to call for it.

JENNY DIVER: You look as if you meant me. Wine is strong enough for me. Indeed, sir, I never drink strong-waters, but when I have the colic.

MACHEATH: Just the excuse of the fine ladies! Why, a lady of quality is never without the colic. I hope, Mrs Coaxer, you have had good success of late in your visits among the mercers.[25]

MRS COAXER: We have so many interlopers[26] – yet with industry, one may still have a little picking. I carried a silver flowered lute string,[27] and a piece of black padesoy[28] to Mr Peachum's lock but last week.

MRS VIXEN: There's Molly Brazen hath the ogle of a rattle snake. She riveted a linen-draper's eye so fast upon her, that he was nicked of three pieces of cambric before he could look off.[29]

MOLLY BRAZEN: O dear madam! But sure nothing can come

---

25. *mercers:* sellers of cloth, particularly of expensive fabrics.

26. *interlopers:* competitors in shoplifting.

27. *lute string:* a fine-quality taffeta.

28. *padesoy:* a type of silk.

29. *There's Molly Brazen . . . look off:* snakes were popularly believed to have the power to hold their victims motionless by the force of their gaze; *ogle:* an amorous glance; *nicked:* cheated; *cambric:* very fine-quality linen.

up to your handling of laces! And then you have such a sweet deluding tongue! To cheat a man is nothing; but the woman must have fine parts[30] indeed who cheats a woman!

MRS VIXEN: Lace, madam, lies in a small compass, and is of easy conveyance. But you are apt, madam, to think too well of your friends.

MRS COAXER: If any woman hath more art than another, to be sure, 'tis Jenny Diver. Though her fellow be never so agreeable, she can pick his pocket as coolly, as if money were her only pleasure. Now that is a command of the passions uncommon in a woman!

JENNY DIVER: I never go to the tavern with a man, but in the view of business. I have other hours, and other sort of men for my pleasure. But had I your address,[31] madam –

MACHEATH: Have done with your compliments, ladies; and drink about.[32] You are not so fond of me, Jenny, as you use to be.

JENNY DIVER: 'Tis not convenient, sir, to show my fondness among so many rivals. 'Tis your own choice, and not the warmth of my inclination that will determine you.

AIR XXIII All in a misty morning

Before the barn door crowing,
The cock by hens attended,
His eyes around him throwing,
Stands for a while suspended.
Then one he singles from the crew,
And cheers the happy hen;
With how do you do, and how do you do,
And how do you do again.

30. *parts:* abilities.
31. *address:* bearing, manner.
32. *drink about:* drink up heartily.

MACHEATH: Ah Jenny! Thou art a dear slut.

DOLLY TRULL: Pray, madam, were you ever in keeping?[33]

SUKY TAWDRY: I hope, madam, I ha'nt been so long upon the town, but I have met with some good fortune as well as my neighbours.

DOLLY TRULL: Pardon me, madam, I meant no harm by the question; 'twas only in the way of conversation.

SUKY TAWDRY: Indeed, madam, if I had not been a fool, I might have lived very handsomely with my last friend. But upon his missing five guineas, he turned me off. Now I never suspected he had counted them.

MRS SLAMMEKIN: Who do you look upon, madam, as your best sort of keepers?

DOLLY TRULL: That, madam, is thereafter as they be.[34]

MRS SLAMMEKIN: I, madam, was once kept by a jew; and bating[35] their religion, to women they are a good sort of people.

SUKY TAWDRY: Now for my part, I own I like an old fellow: for we always make them pay for what they can't do.

MRS VIXEN: A spruce prentice, let me tell you, ladies, is no ill thing, they bleed freely.[36] I have sent at least two or three dozen of them in my time to the plantations.[37]

JENNY DIVER: But to be sure, sir, with so much good fortune as you have had upon the road, you must be grown immensely rich.

MACHEATH: The road, indeed, hath done me justice, but the gaming table hath been my ruin.

33. *in keeping:* kept as a mistress.

34. *That . . . they be:* i.e. 'that depends on how they behave in practice'

35. *bating:* leaving aside.

36. *bleed:* spend money.

37. *I . . . plantations:* supporting Mrs Vixen has ruined the apprentices financially so that they have turned to crime, been caught, and transported to the colonies.

AIR XXIV *When once I lay with another man's wife*

JENNY DIVER:

> *The gamesters and lawyers are jugglers[38] alike,*
> *If they meddle your all is in danger.*
> *Like gypsies, if once they can finger a souse,[39]*
> *Your pockets they pick, and they pilfer your house,*
> *And give your estate to a stranger.*

A man of courage should never put anything to the risk, but his life. These are the tools of a man of honour. Cards and dice are only fit for cowardly cheats, who prey upon their friends. [*She takes up his pistol.* SUKY TAWDRY *takes up the other.*]

SUKY TAWDRY: This, sir, is fitter for your hand. Besides your loss of money, 'tis a loss to the ladies. Gaming takes you off from women. How fond could I be of you! But before company, 'tis ill bred.

MACHEATH: Wanton hussies!

JENNY DIVER: I must and will have a kiss to give my wine a zest.

> [*They take him about the neck, and make signs to*
> PEACHUM *and the constables, who rush in upon him.*]

SCENE V

[*To them,* PEACHUM *and constables.*]

PEACHUM: I seize you, sir, as my prisoner.

MACHEATH: Was this well done, Jenny? Women are decoy ducks; who can trust them! Beasts, jades, jilts, harpies, furies, whores!

PEACHUM: Your case, Mr Macheath, is not particular.[40] The

38. *jugglers*: cheaters.
39. *souse*: a small coin, of very little value.
40. *particular*: unique.

greatest heroes have been ruined by women. But, to do them justice, I must own they are a pretty sort of creatures, if we could trust them. You must now, sir, take your leave of the ladies, and if they have a mind to make you a visit, they will be sure to find you at home. The gentleman, ladies, lodges in Newgate. Constables, wait upon the Captain to his lodgings.

AIR XXV When first I laid siege to my Chloris

MACHEATH: *At the tree I shall suffer with pleasure,*
At the tree I shall suffer with pleasure,
Let me go where I will,
In all kinds of ill,
I shall find no such Furies as these are.

PEACHUM: Ladies, I'll take care the reckoning shall be discharged.

[*Exit* MACHEATH, *guarded with* PEACHUM *and the constables.*]

SCENE VI

[*The women remain.*]

MRS VIXEN: Look ye, Mrs Jenny, though Mr Peachum may have made a private bargain with you and Suky Tawdry for betraying the Captain, as we were all assisting, we ought all to share alike.

MRS COAXER: I think Mr Peachum, after so long an acquaintance, might have trusted me as well as Jenny Diver.

MRS SLAMMEKIN: I am sure at least three men of his hanging, and in a year's time too, (if he did me justice) should be set down to my account.

DOLLY TRULL: Mrs Slammekin, that is not fair. For you know one of them was taken in bed with me.

JENNY DIVER: As far as a bowl of punch or a treat, I believe Mrs Suky will join with me. As for anything else, ladies, you cannot in conscience expect it.

MRS SLAMMEKIN: Dear madam –

DOLLY TRULL: I would not for the world –

MRS SLAMMEKIN: 'Tis impossible for me –

DOLLY TRULL: As I hope to be saved, madam –

MRS SLAMMEKIN: Nay, then I must stay here all night –

DOLLY TRULL: Since you command me.[41]

[*Exeunt with great ceremony.*]

SCENE VII *Newgate*

LOCKIT, *turnkeys*,[42] MACHEATH, *constables*

LOCKIT: Noble Captain, you are welcome. You have not been a lodger of mine this year and half. You know the custom, sir. Garnish,[43] Captain, garnish. Hand me down those fetters there.

MACHEATH: Those, Mr Lockit, seem to be the heaviest of the whole set. With your leave, I should like the further pair better.

LOCKIT: Look ye, Captain, we know what is fittest for our prisoners. When a gentleman uses me with civility, I always do the best I can to please him. Hand them down I say. We have them of all prices, from one guinea to ten, and 'tis fitting every gentleman should please himself.

41. *Dear madam . . . command me:* Mrs Slammekin and Dolly Trull parody the manners of the polite world in insisting that the other take precedence on leaving the tavern.

42. *turnkeys:* jailers.

43. *Garnish:* the system of tips which new prisoners were required to pay to guards and older prisoners on entering the prison. Being imprisoned in Newgate was expensive; see editors' introduction, p. 16.

MACHEATH: I understand you, sir. [*Gives money*.] The fees here are so many, and so exorbitant, that few fortunes can bear the expense of getting off handsomely, or of dying like a gentleman.

LOCKIT: Those, I see, will fit the Captain better. Take down the further pair. Do but examine them, sir. Never was better work. How genteelly they are made! They will sit as easy as a glove, and the nicest[44] man in England might not be ashamed to wear them. [*He puts on the chains*.] If I had the best gentleman in the land in my custody I could not equip him more handsomely. And so, sir – I now leave you to your private meditations.

SCENE VIII

MACHEATH

AIR XXVI Courtiers, courtiers think it no harm

> *Man may escape from rope and gun;*
> *Nay, some have out-lived the doctor's pill;*
> *Who takes a woman must be undone,*
>   *That Basilisk[45] is sure to kill.*
> *The fly that sips treacle is lost in the sweets,*
> *So he that tastes woman, woman, woman,*
>   *He that tastes woman, ruin meets.*

To what a woeful plight have I brought myself! Here must I (all day long, 'till I am hanged) be confined to hear the reproaches of a wench who lays her ruin[46] at my door. I am in the custody of her father, and to be sure if he knows of the matter, I shall have a fine time on't betwixt this and my

44. *nicest*: most fastidious.
45. *Basilisk*: a mythical serpent with the power to kill anything its glance fell upon.
46. *ruin*: seduction.

execution. But I promised the wench marriage. What signifies a promise to a woman? Does not man in marriage itself promise a hundred things that he never means to perform? Do all we can, women will believe us; for they look upon a promise as an excuse for following their own inclinations. But here comes Lucy, and I cannot get from her – would I were deaf!

SCENE IX

MACHEATH, LUCY

LUCY: You base man you – how can you look me in the face after what hath past between us? See here, perfidious wretch, how I am forced to bear about the load of infamy[47] you have laid upon me. O Macheath! Thou hast robbed me of my quiet – to see thee tortured would give me pleasure.

AIR XXVII A lovely lass to a friar came

> *Thus when a good huswife sees a rat*
> *In her trap in the morning taken,*
> *With pleasure her heart goes pit a pat,*
> *In revenge for her loss of bacon.*
> *Then she throws him*
> *To the dog or cat,*
> *To be worried, crushed and shaken.*

MACHEATH: Have you no bowels,[48] no tenderness, my dear Lucy, to see a husband in these circumstances?
LUCY: A husband!
MACHEATH: In every respect but the form, and that, my dear,

47. *how . . . infamy:* Lucy is five months pregnant – see II.XIII ('Hadst thou been hanged five years ago, I had been happy').
48. *bowels:* pity.

may be said over us at any time. Friends should not insist upon ceremonies. From a man of honour, his word is as good as his bond.

LUCY: 'Tis the pleasure of all you fine men to insult the women you have ruined.

AIR XXVIII 'Twas when the sea was roaring

> How cruel are the traitors,
>   Who lie and swear in jest,
> To cheat unguarded creatures
>   Of virtue, fame, and rest!
> Whoever steals a shilling,
>   Through shame the guilt conceals:
> In love the perjured villain
>   With boasts the theft reveals.

MACHEATH: The very first opportunity, my dear, (have but patience) you shall be my wife in whatever manner you please.

LUCY: Insinuating monster! And so you think I know nothing of the affair of Miss Polly Peachum. I could tear thy eyes out!

MACHEATH: Sure Lucy, you can't be such a fool as to be jealous of Polly!

LUCY: Are you not married to her, you brute, you?

MACHEATH: Married! Very good. The wench gives it out only to vex thee, and to ruin me in thy good opinion. 'Tis true, I go to the house; I chat with the girl, I kiss her, I say a thousand things to her (as all gentlemen do) that mean nothing, to divert myself; and now the silly jade hath set it about that I am married to her, to let me know what she would be at. Indeed, my dear Lucy, these violent passions may be of ill consequence to a woman in your condition.

LUCY: Come, come, Captain, for all your assurance, you know that Miss Polly hath put it out of your power to do me the justice you promised me.

MACHEATH: A jealous woman believes everything her passion suggests. To convince you of my sincerity, if we can find the Ordinary,[49] I shall have no scruples of making you my wife; and I know the consequence of having two at a time.

LUCY: That you are only to be hanged, and so get rid of them both.

MACHEATH: I am ready, my dear Lucy, to give you satisfaction – if you think there is any in marriage. What can a man of honour say more?

LUCY: So then it seems, you are not married to Miss Polly.

MACHEATH: You know, Lucy, the girl is prodigiously conceited. No man can say a civil thing to her, but (like other fine ladies) her vanity makes her think he's her own for ever and ever.

AIR XXIX The sun had loosed his weary teams

The first time at the looking-glass
The mother sets her daughter,
The image strikes the smiling lass
With self-love ever after.
Each time she looks, she, fonder grown,
Thinks every charm grows stronger.
But alas, vain maid, all eyes but your own
Can see you are not younger.

When women consider their own beauties, they are all alike unreasonable in their demands; for they expect their lovers should like them as long as they like themselves.

LUCY: Yonder is my father – perhaps this way we may light upon the Ordinary, who shall try if you will be as good as your word. For I long to be made an honest woman.

49. *Ordinary:* the chaplain of Newgate; a clergyman and therefore able to perform marriages.

SCENE X[50]

PEACHUM, LOCKIT *with an account-book*

LOCKIT: In this last affair, Brother Peachum, we are agreed. You have consented to go halves in Macheath.

PEACHUM: We shall never fall out about an execution. But as to that article, pray how stands our last year's account?

LOCKIT: If you will run your eye over it, you'll find 'tis fair and clearly stated.

PEACHUM: This long arrear of the Government is very hard upon us![51] Can it be expected that we should hang our acquaintance for nothing, when our betters will hardly save theirs without being paid for it. Unless the people in employment pay better, I promise them for the future, I shall let other rogues live besides their own.

LOCKIT: Perhaps, brother, they are afraid these matters may be carried too far. We are treated too by them with contempt, as if our profession were not reputable.

PEACHUM: In one respect indeed, our employment may be reckoned dishonest, because, like great statesmen, we encourage those who betray their friends.

LOCKIT: Such language, brother, anywhere else, might turn to your prejudice. Learn to be more guarded, I beg you.

AIR XXX[52] How happy are we

When you censure the age,
Be cautious and sage,

---

50. This scene was understood by contemporary audiences to parody the relationship between Walpole and his brother-in-law Lord Townshend; see editors' introduction, p. 27. A letter from Swift to Gay dated 28 March 1728 suggests that a reference to the quarrel scene between Brutus and Cassius in Shakespeare's *Julius Caesar* (IV.III) may also be intended.

51. *This . . . us:* the forty-pound reward due to those whose evidence led to the conviction and execution of criminals was rarely paid promptly.

52. There is a tradition that Walpole attended an early performance of *The Beggar's Opera*, and that when this Air was sung the audience loudly encored it with their eyes on

> *Lest the courtiers offended should be:*
> *If you mention vice or bribe,*
> *'Tis so pat to all the tribe;*
> *Each cries — That was levelled at me.*

PEACHUM: Here's poor Ned Clincher's name,[53] I see. Sure, brother Lockit, there was a little unfair proceeding in Ned's case: for he told me in the condemned hold,[54] that for value received, you had promised him a Session or two longer without molestation.

LOCKIT: Mr Peachum – this is the first time my honour was ever called in question.

PEACHUM: Business is at an end – if once we act dishonourably.

LOCKIT: Who accuses me?

PEACHUM: You are warm, brother.

LOCKIT: He that attacks my honour, attacks my livelihood. And this usage – sir – is not to be born.

PEACHUM: Since you provoke me to speak – I must tell you too, that Mrs Coaxer charges you with defrauding her of her information-money, for the apprehending of curl-pated Hugh. Indeed, indeed, brother, we must punctually pay our spies, or we shall have no information.

LOCKIT: Is this language to me, sirrah – who have saved you from the gallows, sirrah! [*Collaring each other.*]

PEACHUM: If I am hanged, it shall be for ridding the world of an arrant rascal.

---

the stage box, where the minister was sitting. Walpole dealt with the situation by himself encoring the song a second time, which 'brought the audience into so much good humour with him, that they gave him a general huzza from all parts of the house' (William Cooke, *Memoirs of Charles Macklin*, London, 1804, p. 54). There is no reliable evidence for the truth of this pleasant anecdote.

53. *Ned Clincher:* a clincher was a person distinguished for witty repartee; there is also some evidence that in eighteenth-century criminal slang 'to clinch' meant to silence or render harmless someone, presumably by killing them.

54. *hold:* cell.

LOCKIT: This hand shall do the office of the halter[55] you deserve, and throttle you – you dog!

PEACHUM: Brother, brother – we are both in the wrong – we shall be both losers in the dispute – for you know we have it in our power to hang each other. You should not be so passionate.

LOCKIT: Nor you so provoking.

PEACHUM: 'Tis our mutual interest; 'tis for the interest of the world we should agree. If I said anything, brother, to the prejudice of your character, I ask pardon.

LOCKIT: Brother Peachum – I can forgive as well as resent. Give me your hand. Suspicion does not become a friend.

PEACHUM: I only meant to give you occasion to justify yourself. But I must now step home, for I expect the gentleman about this snuff-box, that Filch nimmed[56] two nights ago in the park. I appointed him at this hour.

SCENE XI

LOCKIT, LUCY

LOCKIT: Whence come you, hussy?

LUCY: My tears might answer that question.

LOCKIT: You have then been whimpering and fondling, like a spaniel, over the fellow that hath abused you.

LUCY: One can't help love; one can't cure it. 'Tis not in my power to obey you, and hate him.

LOCKIT: Learn to bear your husband's death like a reasonable woman. 'Tis not the fashion, nowadays, so much as to affect sorrow upon these occasions. No woman would ever marry, if she had not the chance of mortality for a release. Act like a woman of spirit, hussy, and thank your father for what he is doing.

55. *halter:* noose.
56. *nimmed:* stole.

AIR XXXI Of a noble race was Shenkin

LUCY: *Is then his fate decreed, sir?*
             Such a man can I think of quitting?
             When first we met, so moves me yet,
             O see how my heart is splitting!

LOCKIT: Look ye, Lucy – there is no saving him. So, I think, you must even do like other widows – buy yourself weeds, and be cheerful.

AIR XXXII You'll think e'er many days ensue

             You'll think e'er many days ensue
             This sentence not severe;
             I hang your husband, child, 'tis true,
             But with him hang your care.
             Twang dang dillo dee.

Like a good wife, go moan over your dying husband. That, child, is your duty. Consider, girl, you can't have the man and the money too – so make yourself as easy as you can, by getting all you can from him.

SCENE XII

LUCY, MACHEATH

LUCY: Though the Ordinary was out of the way today, I hope, my dear, you will, upon the first opportunity, quiet my scruples. O sir! My father's hard heart is not to be softened, and I am in the utmost despair.

MACHEATH: But if I could raise a small sum – would not twenty guineas, think you, move him? Of all the arguments in the way of business, the perquisite[57] is the most prevail-

57. *perquisite:* a tip customarily expected for services rendered; in this context it is a polite euphemism for a bribe.

ing. Your father's perquisites for the escape of prisoners must amount to a considerable sum in the year. Money well timed, and properly applied, will do any thing.

AIR XXXIII London ladies

If you at an office solicit your due,[58]
  And would not have matters neglected;
You must quicken the clerk with the perquisite too,
  To do what his duty directed.
Or would you the frowns of a lady prevent,
  She too has this palpable failing,
The perquisite softens her into consent;
  That reason with all is prevailing.

LUCY: What love or money can do shall be done: for all my comfort depends upon your safety.

SCENE XIII

LUCY, MACHEATH, POLLY

POLLY: Where is my dear husband? Was a rope ever intended for this neck! O let me throw my arms about it, and throttle thee with love! Why dost thou turn away from me? 'Tis thy Polly. 'Tis thy wife.

MACHEATH: Was ever such an unfortunate rascal as I am!

LUCY: Was there ever such another villain!

POLLY: O Macheath! Was it for this we parted? Taken! Imprisoned! Tried! Hanged! Cruel reflection! I'll stay with thee 'till death. No force shall tear thy dear wife from thee now. What means my love? Not one kind word! Not one kind look! Think what thy Polly suffers to see thee in this condition.

---

58. *your due:* that which is rightly or justly yours.

AIR XXXIV All in the downs

Thus when the swallow, seeking prey,
  Within the sash[59] is closely pent,
His consort, with bemoaning lay,[60]
  Without sits pining for th' event.
Her chattering lovers all around her skim;
  She heeds them not (poor bird!) her soul's with him.

MACHEATH [*aside*]: I must disown her. The wench is distracted.

LUCY: Am I then bilked[61] of my virtue? Can I have no reparation? Sure men were born to lie, and women to believe them! O villain! Villain!

POLLY: Am I not thy wife? Thy neglect of me, thy aversion to me too severely proves it. Look on me. Tell me, am I not thy wife?

LUCY: Perfidious wretch!

POLLY: Barbarous husband!

LUCY: Hadst thou been hanged five months ago, I had been happy.

POLLY: And I too. If you had been kind to me 'till death, it would not have vexed me – and that's no very unreasonable request, (though from a wife) to a man who hath not above seven or eight days to live.

LUCY: Art thou then married to another? Hast thou two wives, monster?

MACHEATH: If women's tongues can cease for an answer – hear me.

LUCY: I won't. Flesh and blood can't bear my usage.

POLLY: Shall I not claim my own? Justice bids me speak.

---

59. *Within the sash:* inside the window.
60. *lay:* song.
61. *bilked:* cheated.

AIR XXXV[62] Have you heard of a frolicsome ditty

MACHEATH: *How happy could I be with either,*
Were t'other dear charmer away!
But while you thus tease me together,
To neither a word will I say;
But tol de rol, etc.

POLLY: Sure, my dear, there ought to be some preference shown to a wife! At least she may claim the appearance of it. He must be distracted with his misfortunes, or he could not use me thus!

LUCY: O villain, villain! Thou hast deceived me – I could even inform against thee with pleasure. Not a prude wishes more heartily to have facts[63] against her intimate acquaintance, than I now wish to have facts against thee. I would have her satisfaction, and they should all out.

AIR XXXVI Irish trot

POLLY: *I'm bubbled.*[64]
LUCY: *– I'm bubbled.*
POLLY: *O how I am troubled!*
LUCY: *Bamboozled, and bit!*[65]
POLLY: *– My distresses are doubled.*
LUCY: *When you come to the tree, should the hangman refuse,*
These fingers, with pleasure, could fasten the noose.
POLLY: *I'm bubbled, etc.*

MACHEATH: Be pacified, my dear Lucy. This is all a fetch[66] of

62. This Air probably alludes to the triangular relationship between Walpole, Lady Walpole, and Maria Skerret, Walpole's mistress; see editors' introduction, p. 27.

63. *facts:* discreditable information; 'evil deed' or 'crime' was the most common meaning of the word 'fact' in the early eighteenth century – it survives in the legal term 'accessory after the fact'.

64. *bubbled:* cheated.

65. *bit:* tricked.

66. *fetch:* ruse.

Polly's, to make me desperate with you in case I get off.[67] If I am hanged, she would fain have the credit of being thought my widow. Really, Polly, this is no time for a dispute of this sort; for whenever you are talking of marriage, I am thinking of hanging.

POLLY: And hast thou the heart to persist in disowning me?

MACHEATH: And hast thou the heart to persist in persuading me that I am married? Why, Polly, dost thou seek to aggravate my misfortunes?

LUCY: Really, Miss Peachum, you but expose yourself. Besides, 'tis barbarous in you to worry a gentleman in his circumstances.

AIR XXXVII

POLLY:

> Cease your funning;
> Force or cunning
> Never shall my heart trapan.[68]
> All these sallies
> Are but malice
> To seduce my constant man.
> 'Tis most certain,
> By their flirting
> Women oft' have envy shown;
> Pleased, to ruin
> Others wooing;
> Never happy in their own!

Decency, madam, methinks might teach you to behave yourself with some reserve with the husband, while his wife is present.

MACHEATH: But seriously, Polly, this is carrying the joke a little too far.

LUCY: If you are determined, madam, to raise a disturbance in

67. to make . . . off: to make you think badly of me if I'm acquitted.
68. trapan: ensnare, beguile.

the prison, I shall be obliged to send for the turnkey to show you the door. I am sorry, madam, you force me to be so ill-bred.

POLLY: Give me leave to tell you, madam: These forward airs don't become you in the least, madam. And my duty, madam, obliges me to stay with my husband, madam.

AIR XXXVIII Good-morrow, gossip Joan

LUCY: *Why how now, Madam Flirt?*
              If you thus must chatter;
           And are for flinging dirt,
              Let's try who best can spatter;
                          Madam Flirt!

POLLY: *Why how now, saucy jade;*
              Sure the wench is tipsy!
[*To him.*]   *How can you see me made*
              The scoff of such a gipsy?
[*To her.*]   *Saucy jade!*

SCENE XIV

LUCY, MACHEATH, POLLY, PEACHUM

PEACHUM: Where's my wench? Ah hussy! Hussy! Come you home, you slut; and when your fellow is hanged, hang yourself, to make your family some amends.

POLLY: Dear, dear father, do not tear me from him. I must speak; I have more to say to him – O! Twist thy fetters about me, that he may not haul me from thee!

PEACHUM: Sure all women are alike! If ever they commit the folly, they are sure to commit another by exposing themselves. Away – not a word more. You are my prisoner now, hussy.

AIR XXXIX Irish howl

POLLY: *No power on earth can e'er divide,*
             The knot that sacred love hath tied.
             When parents draw against our mind,
             The true-love's knot they faster bind.
                  Oh, oh ray, oh Amborah – oh, oh, etc.

[*Holding* MACHEATH, PEACHUM *pulling her.*]

SCENE XV

LUCY, MACHEATH

MACHEATH: I am naturally compassionate, wife; so that I could not use the wench as she deserved; which made you at first suspect there was something in what she said.

LUCY: Indeed, my dear, I was strangely puzzled.

MACHEATH: If that had been the case, her father would never have brought me into this circumstance. No, Lucy, I had rather die than be false to thee.

LUCY: How happy am I, if you say this from your heart! For I love thee so, that I could sooner bear to see thee hanged than in the arms of another.

MACHEATH: But couldst thou bear to see me hanged?

LUCY: O Macheath, I can never live to see that day.

MACHEATH: You see, Lucy; in the account of love you are in my debt, and you must now be convinced, that I rather choose to die than be another's. Make me, if possible, love thee more, and let me owe my life to thee. If you refuse to assist me, Peachum and your father will immediately put me beyond all means of escape.

LUCY: My father, I know, hath been drinking hard with the prisoners:[69] and I fancy he is now taking his nap in his own

69. *My father . . . prisoners:* alcohol was freely available and widely consumed in Newgate, as in all eighteenth-century prisons.

room. If I can procure the keys, shall I go off with thee, my dear?

MACHEATH: If we are together, 'twill be impossible to lie concealed. As soon as the search begins to be a little cool, I will send to thee. 'Till then my heart is thy prisoner.

LUCY: Come then, my dear husband – owe thy life to me. And though you love me not – be grateful. But that Polly runs in my head strangely.

MACHEATH: A moment of time may make us unhappy for-ever.

AIR XL The lass of Patie's mill

LUCY:
I like the fox shall grieve,
  Whose mate hath left her side,
Whom hounds, from morn to eve,
  Chase o'er the country wide.
Where can my lover hide?
  Where cheat the weary pack?
If love be not his guide,
  He never will come back!

ACT III

LOCKIT, LUCY

LOCKIT: To be sure, wench, you must have been aiding and abetting to help him to this escape.

LUCY: Sir, here hath been Peachum and his daughter Polly, and to be sure they know the ways of Newgate as well as if they had been born and bred in the place all their lives. Why must all your suspicion light upon me?

LOCKIT: Lucy, Lucy, I will have none of these shuffling answers.

LUCY: Well then – if I know anything of him I wish I may be burnt![1]

LOCKIT: Keep your temper, Lucy, or I shall pronounce you guilty.

LUCY: Keep yours, sir. I do wish I may be burnt. I do – and what can I say more to convince you?

LOCKIT: Did he tip handsomely? How much did he come down with? Come hussy, don't cheat your father; and I shall not be angry with you. Perhaps, you have made a better bargain with him than I could have done. How much, my good girl?

LUCY: You know, sir, I am fond of him, and would have given money to have kept him with me.

LOCKIT: Ah Lucy! Thy education might have put thee more

---

1. *burnt*: burning to death was the punishment prescribed for women found guilty of treason. Or Lucy may be referring to the fact that first offenders who successfully pleaded benefit of clergy were branded on the thumb so as to ensure that they couldn't use the plea again.

upon thy guard; for a girl in the bar of an ale-house is always besieged.

LUCY: Dear sir, mention not my education – for 'twas to that I owe my ruin.

AIR XLI If love's a sweet passion

When young at the bar you first taught me to score,
And bid me be free of my lips, and no more;
I was kissed by the parson, the squire, and the sot.
When the guest was departed, the kiss was forgot.
But his kiss was so sweet, and so closely he pressed,
That I languished and pined 'till I granted the rest.

If you can forgive me, sir, I will make a fair confession, for to be sure he hath been a most barbarous villain to me.

LOCKIT: And so you have let him escape, hussy – have you?

LUCY: When a woman loves, a kind look, a tender word can persuade her to anything. And I could ask no other bribe.

LOCKIT: Thou wilt always be a vulgar slut, Lucy. If you would not be looked upon as a fool, you should never do anything but upon the foot of interest. Those that act otherwise are their own bubbles.[2]

LUCY: But love, sir, is a misfortune that may happen to the most discreet woman, and in love we are all fools alike. Notwithstanding all he swore, I am now fully convinced that Polly Peachum is actually his wife. Did I let him escape, (fool that I was!) to go to her? Polly will wheedle herself into his money, and then Peachum will hang him, and cheat us both.

LOCKIT: So I am to be ruined, because, forsooth, you must be in love! A very pretty excuse!

LUCY: I could murder that impudent happy strumpet: I gave him his life, and that creature enjoys the sweets of it. Ungrateful Macheath!

2. *bubbles:* dupes.

AIR XLII South-Sea ballad

My love is all madness and folly,
  Alone I lie,
  Toss, tumble, and cry,
What a happy creature is Polly!
Was e'er such a wretch as I!
With rage I redden like scarlet,
That my dear inconstant varlet,
  Stark blind to my charms,
  Is lost in the arms
Of that jilt, that inveigling harlot!
  Stark blind to my charms,
  Is lost in the arms
Of that jilt, that inveigling harlot!
This, this my resentment alarms.

LOCKIT: And so, after all this mischief, I must stay here to be entertained with your caterwauling, Mistress Puss! Out of my sight, wanton strumpet! You shall fast and mortify yourself into reason, with now and then a little handsome discipline to bring you to your senses. Go.

SCENE II

LOCKIT

Peachum then intends to outwit me in this affair; but I'll be even with him. The dog is leaky[3] in his liquor, so I'll ply him that way, get the secret from him, and turn this affair to my own advantage. Lions, wolves, and vultures don't live together in herds, droves or flocks. Of all animals of prey, man is the only sociable one. Every one of us preys upon his

3. *leaky*: garrulous.

neighbour, and yet we herd together. Peachum is
panion, my friend – according to the custom of the w
indeed, he may quote thousands of precedents for cheat.
me. And shall not I make use of the privilege of friendship to
make him a return?

AIR XLIII Packington's pound

> *Thus gamesters united in friendship are found,*
> *Though they know that their industry all is a cheat;*
> *They flock to their prey at the dice-box's sound,*
> *And join to promote one another's deceit.*
>> *But if by mishap*
>> *They fail of a chap,*[4]
> *To keep in their hands, they each other entrap.*
> *Like pikes, lank with hunger, who miss of their ends,*
> *They bite their companions, and prey on their friends.*

Now, Peachum, you and I, like honest tradesmen, are to
have a fair trial which of us two can over-reach the other.
Lucy! [*Enter* LUCY.] Are there any of Peachum's people now
in the house?

LUCY: Filch, sir, is drinking a quartern of strong-waters[5] in the
next room with Black Moll.

LOCKIT: Bid him come to me.

SCENE III

LOCKIT, FILCH

LOCKIT: Why, boy, thou lookest as if thou wert half starved;
like a shotten herring.[6]

---

4. *chap:* customer; here in the sense of 'victim'.

5. *quartern:* a quarter of a pint; *strong waters:* any distilled spirit; at this period the phrase
usually connoted gin.

6. *shotten herring:* a herring after spawning – thin and exhausted.

FILCH: One had need have the constitution of a horse to go through the business. Since the favourite child-getter[7] was disabled by a mishap,[8] I have picked up a little money by helping the ladies to a pregnancy against their being called down to sentence. But if a man cannot get an honest livelihood any easier way, I am sure 'tis what I can't undertake for another Session.

LOCKIT: Truly, if that great man should tip off,[9] 'twould be an irreparable loss. The vigour and prowess of a knight-errant never saved half the ladies in distress that he hath done. But, boy, can'st thou tell me where thy master is to be found?

FILCH: At his lock,[10] sir, at the Crooked Billet.

LOCKIT: Very well. I have nothing more with you. [*Exit* FILCH.] I'll go to him there, for I have many important affairs to settle with him; and in the way of those transactions, I'll artfully get into his secret. So that Macheath shall not remain a day longer out of my clutches.

SCENE IV   *A gaming-house*

MACHEATH *in a fine tarnished coat*,[11] BEN BUDGE, MATT OF THE MINT

MACHEATH: I am sorry, gentlemen, the road was so barren of money. When my friends are in difficulties, I am always glad that my fortune can be serviceable to them. [*Gives them money*.] You see, gentlemen, I am not a mere court friend, who professes everything and will do nothing.

---

7. *child-getter*: as women convicted of capital crimes could not be hung if they could prove that they were pregnant, it was clearly in the interests of females awaiting trial in Newgate to become so.

8. *a mishap*: presumably venereal disease.

9. *tip off*: die.

10. *lock*: warehouse where stolen goods were stored.

11. *a fine tarnished coat*: i.e. a coat of fine quality, but faded.

AIR XLIV Lillibullero

The modes of the court so common are grown,
  That a true friend can hardly be met;
Friendship for interest is but a loan,
  Which they let out for what they can get.
    'Tis true, you find
    Some friends so kind,
Who will give you good counsel themselves to defend.
    In sorrowful ditty,
    They promise, they pity,
But shift you for money, from friend to friend.

But we, gentlemen, have still honour enough to break through the corruptions of the world. And while I can serve you, you may command me.

BEN BUDGE: It grieves my heart that so generous a man should be involved in such difficulties, as oblige him to live with such ill company, and herd with gamesters.

MATT OF THE MINT: See the partiality of mankind! One man may steal a horse, better than another look over a hedge.[12] Of all mechanics,[13] of all servile handycrafts-men, a gamester is the vilest. But yet, as many of the quality are of the profession, he is admitted amongst the politest company. I wonder we are not more respected.

MACHEATH: There will be deep play[14] tonight at Marybone, and consequently money may be picked up upon the road. Meet me there, and I'll give you the hint who is worth setting.[15]

MATT OF THE MINT: The fellow with a brown coat with a narrow gold binding,[16] I am told, is never without money.

12. *One man . . . hedge:* an old proverb; the sense is that some people can get away with anything, while others are always in trouble however innocent they are.

13. *mechanics:* manual workers.

14. *deep play:* gambling for high stakes.

15. *setting:* setting upon, robbery.

16. *binding:* edging.

MACHEATH: What do you mean, Matt? Sure you will not think of meddling with him! He's a good honest kind of a fellow, and one of us.

BEN BUDGE: To be sure, sir, we will put ourselves under your direction.

MACHEATH: Have an eye upon the money-lenders. A rouleau,[17] or two, would prove a pretty sort of an expedition. I hate extortion.

MATT OF THE MINT: Those rouleaus are very pretty things. I hate your bank bills: there is such a hazard in putting them off.

MACHEATH: There is a certain man of distinction, who in his time hath nicked[18] me out of a great deal of the ready. He is in my cash,[19] Ben: I'll point him out to you this evening, and you shall draw upon him for the debt. The company are met; I hear the dice-box in the other room. So, gentlemen, your servant. You'll meet me at Marybone.

SCENE V *Peachum's Lock*

A table with wine, brandy, pipes and tobacco

PEACHUM, LOCKIT

LOCKIT: The Coronation account,[20] brother Peachum, is of so intricate a nature, that I believe it will never be settled.

PEACHUM: It consists indeed of a great variety of articles. It was worth to our people, in fees of different kinds, above ten

---

17. *rouleau:* a quantity of gold coins, from twenty to fifty or more, wrapped in rolls of paper; they were used as stakes at gambling tables.

18. *nicked . . . ready:* won large sums of money from me at dice; 'nicked' in this context may also imply cheating.

19. *He is in my cash:* i.e. his money is really mine.

20. *Coronation account:* i.e. the account of goods stolen during the Coronation of George II in October 1727.

instalments.[21] This is part of the account, brother, that lies open before us.

LOCKIT: A lady's tail[22] of rich brocade – that, I see, is disposed of.

PEACHUM: To Mrs Diana Trapes, the tally-woman,[23] and she will make a good hand on't in shoes and slippers, to trick out young ladies, upon their going into keeping.[24]

LOCKIT: But I don't see any article of the jewels.

PEACHUM: Those are so well known, that they must be sent abroad – you'll find them entered under the article of Exportation. As for the snuff-boxes, watches, swords, etc. – I thought it best to enter them under their several heads.

LOCKIT: Seven and twenty women's pockets[25] complete, with the several things therein contained; all sealed, numbered, and entered.

PEACHUM: But, brother, it is impossible for us now to enter upon this affair. We should have the whole day before us. Besides, the account of the last half year's plate[26] is in a book by itself, which lies at the other office.

LOCKIT: Bring us then more liquor. Today shall be for pleasure – tomorrow for business. Ah brother, those daughters of ours are two slippery hussies. Keep a watchful eye upon Polly, and Macheath in a day or two shall be our own again.

21. *instalments:* days when a new Lord Mayor of London was installed; like a coronation, a day when large crowds of well-dressed people gathered and the opportunities for robbery were therefore good.

22. *tail:* train; an extension of the gown that trails over the ground.

23. *tally-woman:* Mrs Trapes rents expensive clothes to prostitutes so that they can ply their trade more effectively.

24. *upon . . . keeping:* i.e. when they become someone's mistress.

25. *women's pockets:* small bags, like modern purses; they were tied round the waist and were frequently a target for thieves.

26. *plate:* silver or gold table ware.

AIR XLV Down in the North Country

What gudgeons[27] are we men!
  Every woman's easy prey.
Though we have felt the hook, again
  We bite and they betray.

The bird that hath been trapped,
  When he hears his calling mate,
To her he flies, again he's clapped
  Within the wiry grate.[28]

PEACHUM: But what signifies catching the bird, if your daughter Lucy will set open the door of the cage?

LOCKIT: If men were answerable for the follies and frailties of their wives and daughters, no friends could keep a good correspondence[29] together for two days. This is unkind of you, brother; for among good friends, what they say or do goes for nothing.

[*Enter a* SERVANT.]

SERVANT: Sir, here's Mrs Diana Trapes wants to speak with you.

PEACHUM: Shall we admit her, brother Lockit?

LOCKIT: By all means. She's a good customer, and a fine-spoken woman. And a woman who drinks and talks so freely, will enliven the conversation.

PEACHUM: Desire her to walk in.

[*Exit* SERVANT.]

27. *gudgeons:* small fish easily caught by anglers; hence gullible people.
28. *grate:* cage.
29. *keep . . . correspondence:* maintain good relations.

SCENE VI

PEACHUM, LOCKIT, MRS TRAPES

PEACHUM: Dear Mrs Dye, your servant. One may know by your kiss, that your gin is excellent.

MRS TRAPES: I was always very curious in[30] my liquors.

LOCKIT: There is no perfumed breath like it. I have been long acquainted with the flavour of those lips, han't I, Mrs Dye?

MRS TRAPES: Fill it up. I take as large draughts of liquor, as I did of love. I hate a flincher in either.

AIR XLVI A shepherd kept sheep

In the days of my youth I could bill like a dove, fa, la, la, etc.
Like a sparrow[31] at all times was ready for love, fa, la, la, etc.
The life of all mortals in kissing should pass,
Lip to lip while we're young – then the lip to the glass, fa, etc.

But now, Mr Peachum, to our business. If you have blacks[32] of any kind, brought in of late; mantoes[33] – velvet scarfs – petticoats – let it be what it will – I am your chap.[34] For all my ladies are very fond of mourning.

PEACHUM: Why, look ye, Mrs Dye – you deal so hard with us, that we can afford to give the gentlemen, who venture their lives for the goods, little or nothing.

MRS TRAPES: The hard times oblige me to go very near in my dealing. To be sure, of late years I have been a great sufferer by the Parliament – three thousand pounds would hardly make me amends. The Act for destroying the Mint,[35] was a

30. *curious in:* fastidious about.

31. *sparrow:* sparrows were traditionally supposed to be lecherous.

32. *blacks:* mourning clothes.

33. *mantoes:* mantuas; gowns with long trains, worn on formal occasions.

34. *chap:* customer.

35. *The Act for destroying the Mint:* the Mint was a district in Southwark which since medieval times had had a quasi-legal status as a sanctuary for debtors and criminals; an Act to remove this and to bring the district more effectively under the control of the law had been passed in 1722.

severe cut upon our business. 'Till then, if a customer stepped out of the way – we knew where to have her. No doubt you know Mrs Coaxer – there's a wench now ('till today) with a good suit of clothes of mine upon her back, and I could never set eyes upon her for three months together. Since the Act too against imprisonment for small sums,[36] my loss there too hath been very considerable, and it must be so, when a lady can borrow[37] a handsome petticoat, or a clean gown, and I not have the least hank upon[38] her! And, o' my conscience, now-a-days most ladies take a delight in cheating, when they can do it with safety.

PEACHUM: Madam, you had a handsome gold watch of us t'other day for seven guineas. Considering we must have our profit, to a gentleman upon the road, a gold watch will be scarce worth the taking.

MRS TRAPES: Consider, Mr Peachum, that watch was remarkable,[39] and not of very safe sale. If you have any black velvet scarfs, they are a handsome winter-wear; and take with most gentlemen who deal with my customers.[40] 'Tis I that put the ladies upon a good foot. 'Tis not youth or beauty that fixes their price. The gentlemen always pay according to their dress, from half a crown to two guineas; and yet those hussies make nothing of bilking of me.[41] Then too, allowing for accidents – I have eleven fine customers now down under the surgeon's hands[42] – what with fees and other expenses, there are great goings-out, and no comings-in,

36. *Act . . . sums:* an Act passed in 1725, designed to prevent imprisonment for debts of less than ten pounds in a superior court or forty shillings in an inferior court. Before the passage of this act, Mrs Trapes could have had a customer who owed her any amount, however small, arrested for debt.

37. *borrow:* hire.

38. *hank upon:* hold over.

39. *remarkable:* easily recognizable.

40. *customers:* Mrs Trapes's 'customers' are prostitutes.

41. *bilking of:* cheating.

42. *now . . . hands:* i.e. with venereal disease.

and not a farthing to pay for at least a month's clothing. We run great risks – great risks indeed.

PEACHUM: As I remember, you said something just now of Mrs Coaxer.

MRS TRAPES: Yes, sir. To be sure I stripped her of a suit of my own clothes about two hours ago; and have left her as she should be, in her shift, with a lover of hers at my house. She called him upstairs, as he was going to Marybone in a hackney coach. And I hope, for her own sake and mine, she will persuade the Captain to redeem her, for the Captain is very generous to the ladies.

LOCKIT: What Captain?

MRS TRAPES: He thought I did not know him. An intimate acquaintance of yours, Mr Peachum. Only Captain Macheath – as fine as a lord.

PEACHUM: Tomorrow, dear Mrs Dye, you shall set your own price upon any of the goods you like. We have at least half a dozen velvet scarfs, and all at your service. Will you give me leave to make you a present of this suit of night-clothes[43] for your own wearing? But are you sure it is Captain Macheath?

MRS TRAPES: Though he thinks I have forgot him, nobody knows him better. I have taken a great deal of the Captain's money in my time at second-hand, for he always loved to have his ladies well dressed.

PEACHUM: Mr Lockit and I have a little business with the Captain – you understand me – and we will satisfy you for Mrs Coaxer's debt.

LOCKIT: Depend upon it – we will deal like men of honour.

MRS TRAPES: I don't enquire after your affairs, so whatever happens, I wash my hands on't. It hath always been my maxim, that one friend should assist another. But if you please – I'll take one of the scarfs home with me. 'Tis always good to have something in hand.

43. *night-clothes:* informal morning or evening attire

SCENE VII　*Newgate*[44]

LUCY

Jealousy, rage, love and fear are at once tearing me to pieces. How I am weather-beaten and shattered with distresses!

AIR XLVII　One evening, having lost my way

> I'm like a skiff on the ocean tossed,
>> Now high, now low, with each billow born,
> With her rudder broke, and her anchor lost,
>> Deserted and all forlorn.
> While thus I lie rolling and tossing all night,
> That Polly lies sporting on seas of delight!
>> Revenge, revenge, revenge,
> Shall appease my restless sprite.

I have the rats-bane[45] ready. I run no risk; for I can lay her death upon the gin, and so many die of that naturally that I shall never be called in question.[46] But say I were to be hanged – I never could be hanged for anything that would give me greater comfort, than the poisoning that slut.

[*Enter* FILCH.]

FILCH: Madam, here's our Miss Polly come to wait upon you.

LUCY: Show her in.

---

44. The romantic motifs and florid language common in the Italian opera are parodied in this scene and the three following.

45. *rats-bane:* rat poison; melodramatic prison scenes involving poisoned cups were common in Italian opera; they occur in Handel's *Radamisto* (1720), *Floridante* (1721), and *Tamerlano* (1724), for example.

46. *I can . . . question:* much of the cheap gin sold in London in the 1720s was improperly distilled and therefore literally poisonous.

SCENE VIII

LUCY, POLLY

LUCY: Dear madam, your servant. I hope you will pardon my passion, when I was so happy to see you last. I was so over-run with the spleen,[47] that I was perfectly out of myself. And really when one hath the spleen, everything is to be excused by a friend.

AIR XLVIII Now Roger, I'll tell thee, because thou'rt my son

> *When a wife's in her pout,*
> *(As she's sometimes, no doubt;)*
> *The good husband as meek as a lamb,*
> *Her vapours[48] to still,*
> *First grants her her will,*
> *And the quieting draught is a dram.*
> *Poor man! And the quieting draught is a dram.*

I wish all our quarrels might have so comfortable a reconciliation.

POLLY: I have no excuse for my own behaviour, madam, but my misfortunes. And really, madam, I suffer too upon your account.

LUCY: But, Miss Polly, in the way of friendship, will you give me leave to propose a glass of cordial to you?

POLLY: Strong-waters are apt to give me the headache. I hope, madam, you will excuse me.

LUCY: Not the greatest lady in the land could have better in her closet,[49] for her own private drinking. You seem mighty low in spirits, my dear.

POLLY: I am sorry, madam, my health will not allow me to

47. *the spleen*: sullenness and low spirits; affecting to have the spleen was fashionable in the early eighteenth century.

48. *vapours*: bad temper.

49. *closet*: private room.

accept of your offer. I should not have left you in the rude manner I did when we met last, madam, had not my papa hauled me away so unexpectedly. I was indeed somewhat provoked, and perhaps might use some expressions that were disrespectful. But really, madam, the Captain treated me with so much contempt and cruelty, that I deserved your pity, rather than your resentment.

LUCY: But since his escape, no doubt all matters are made up again. Ah Polly! Polly! 'Tis I am the unhappy wife; and he loves you as if you were only his mistress.

POLLY: Sure, madam, you cannot think me so happy as to be the object of your jealousy. A man is always afraid of a woman who loves him too well, so that I must expect to be neglected and avoided.

LUCY: Then our cases, my dear Polly, are exactly alike. Both of us indeed have been too fond.

AIR XLIX O Bessy Bell

POLLY:	*A curse attends that woman's love,*
	Who always would be pleasing.
LUCY:	*The pertness[50] of the billing dove,*
	Like tickling, is but teasing.
POLLY:	*What then in love can woman do?*
LUCY:	*If we grow fond they shun us.*
POLLY:	*And when we fly them, they pursue.*
LUCY:	*But leave us when they've won us.*

Love is so very whimsical in both sexes, that it is impossible to be lasting. But my heart is particular,[51] and contradicts my own observation.

POLLY: But really, Mistress Lucy, by his last behaviour, I think I ought to envy you. When I was forced from him, he did not

50. *pertness:* sauciness.
51. *particular:* devoted solely to one man.

show the least tenderness; but perhaps, he hath a heart not capable of it.

AIR L　Would Fate to me Belinda give

> *Among the men, coquettes we find,*
> *Who court by turns all womankind;*
> *And we grant all their hearts desired,*
> *When they are flattered, and admired.*

The coquettes of both sexes are self-lovers, and that is a love no other whatever can dispossess. I fear, my dear Lucy, our husband is one of those.

LUCY: Away with these melancholy reflections. Indeed, my dear Polly, we are both of us a cup too low. Let me prevail upon you, to accept of my offer.

AIR LI　Come, sweet lass

> *Come sweet lass,*
> *Let's banish sorrow*
> *'Till tomorrow;*
> *Come, sweet lass,*
> *Let's take a chirping[52] glass.*
> *Wine can clear*
> *The vapours of despair;*
> *And make us light as air;*
> *Then drink, and banish care.*

I can't bear, child, to see you in such low spirits. And I must persuade you to what I know will do you good. [*Aside.*] I shall now soon be even with the hypocritical strumpet.

52. *chirping*: cheering.

SCENE IX

POLLY

All this wheedling of Lucy cannot be for nothing. At this time too! When I know she hates me! The dissembling of a woman is always the forerunner of mischief. By pouring strong-waters down my throat, she thinks to pump some secrets out of me. I'll be upon my guard, and won't taste a drop of her liquor, I'm resolved.

SCENE X

LUCY, *with strong-waters.* POLLY

LUCY: Come, Miss Polly.

POLLY: Indeed, child, you have given yourself trouble to no purpose. You must, my dear, excuse me.

LUCY: Really, Miss Polly, you are so squeamishly affected about taking a cup of strong-waters as a lady before company. I vow, Polly, I shall take it monstrously ill if you refuse me. Brandy and men (though women love them never so well) are always taken by us with some reluctance – unless 'tis in private.

POLLY: I protest, madam, it goes against me. What do I see! Macheath again in custody! Now every glimmering of happiness is lost. [*Drops the glass of liquor on the ground.*]

LUCY [*aside*]: Since things are thus, I'm glad the wench hath escaped: for by this event, 'tis plain, she was not happy enough to deserve to be poisoned.

SCENE XI

LOCKIT, MACHEATH, PEACHUM, LUCY, POLLY

LOCKIT: Set your heart to rest, Captain. You have neither the chance of love or money for another escape, for you are ordered to be called down upon your trial immediately.

PEACHUM: Away, hussies! This is not a time for a man to be hampered with his wives. You see, the gentleman is in chains already.

LUCY: O husband, husband, my heart longed to see thee; but to see thee thus distracts me!

POLLY: Will not my dear husband look upon his Polly? Why hadst thou not flown to me for protection? With me thou hadst been safe.

AIR LII *The last time I went o'er the moor*

POLLY: *Hither, dear husband, turn your eyes.*
LUCY: *Bestow one glance to cheer me.*
POLLY: *Think with that look, thy Polly dies.*
LUCY: *O shun me not – but hear me.*
POLLY: *'Tis Polly sues.*
LUCY: *– 'Tis Lucy speaks.*
POLLY: *Is thus true love requited?*
LUCY: *My heart is bursting.*
POLLY: *– Mine too breaks.*
LUCY: *Must I –*
POLLY: *– Must I be slighted?*

MACHEATH: What would you have me say, ladies? You see, this affair will soon be at an end, without my disobliging either of you.

PEACHUM: But the settling this point, Captain, might prevent a law-suit between your two widows.

AIR LIII   Tom Tinker's my true love

MACHEATH:

> *Which way shall I turn me?*[53] *How can I decide?*
> *Wives, the day of our death, are as fond as a bride.*
> *One wife is too much for most husbands to hear,*
> *But two at a time there's no mortal can bear.*
> *This way, and that way, and which way I will,*
> *What would comfort the one, t'other wife would take ill.*

POLLY: But if his own misfortunes have made him insensible to mine, a father sure will be more compassionate. Dear, dear sir, sink[54] the material evidence, and bring him off at his trial – Polly upon her knees begs it of you.

AIR LIV   I am a poor shepherd undone

> *When my hero in court appears,*
>   *And stands arraigned for his life;*
> *Then think of poor Polly's tears;*
>   *For ah! Poor Polly's his wife.*
> *Like the sailor he holds up his hand,*
>   *Distressed on the dashing wave.*
> *To die a dry death at land,*
>   *Is as bad as a wat'ry grave.*
> *And alas, poor Polly!*
> *Alack, and well-a-day!*
> *Before I was in love,*
>   *O! every month was May.*

LUCY: If Peachum's heart is hardened; sure you, sir, will have more compassion on a daughter. I know the evidence

---

53. *Which way shall I turn me?:* Macheath's question echoes Marc Antony's line 'Oh, Dollabella, which way shall I turn' (III.379) from Dryden's heroic tragedy *All for Love* (1677). Antony is confronted with a choice between his wife, Octavia, and his great love Cleopatra – a tragic conflict between duty and desire. Macheath's position, torn between Polly and Lucy, burlesques Antony's.

54. *sink:* suppress

is in your power: how then can you be a tyrant to me? [*Kneeling.*]

AIR LV Ianthe the lovely

When he holds up his hand arraigned for his life,
O think of your daughter, and think I'm his wife!
What are cannons, or bombs, or clashing of swords?
For death is more certain by witnesses words.
Then nail up their lips; that dread thunder allay;
And each month of my life will hereafter be May.

LOCKIT: Macheath's time is come, Lucy. We know our own affairs, therefore let us have no more whimpering or whining.

AIR LVI A cobbler there was

Ourselves, like the great, to secure a retreat,
When matters require it, must give up our gang:
  And good reason why,
  Or, instead of the fry,
  Even Peachum and I,
Like poor petty rascals, might hang, hang;
Like poor petty rascals, might hang.

PEACHUM: Set your heart at rest, Polly. Your husband is to die today. Therefore, if you are not already provided, 'tis high time to look about for another. There's comfort for you, you slut.

LOCKIT: We are ready, sir, to conduct you to the Old Bailey.

AIR LVII Bonny Dundee

MACHEATH:
  The charge is prepared; the lawyers are met,
  The judges all ranged (a terrible show!)
  I go, undismayed. For death is a debt,

A debt on demand. So, take what I owe.
Then farewell my love – dear charmers, adieu.
Contented I die – 'tis the better for you.
Here ends all dispute the rest of our lives.
For this way at once I please all my wives.

Now, gentlemen, I am ready to attend you.

SCENE XII

LUCY, POLLY, FILCH

POLLY: Follow them, Filch, to the court. And when the trial is over, bring me a particular[55] account of his behaviour, and of everything that happened. You'll find me here with Miss Lucy. [*Exit* FILCH.] But why is all this music?

LUCY: The prisoners, whose trials are put off till next Session, are diverting themselves.

POLLY: Sure there is nothing so charming as music! I'm fond of it to distraction! But alas! Now, all mirth seems an insult upon my affliction. Let us retire, my dear Lucy, and indulge our sorrows. The noisy crew, you see, are coming upon us.

[*Exeunt.*]

A Dance of Prisoners in Chains, etc.

SCENE XIII   *The condemned hold*[56]

MACHEATH, *in a melancholy posture*

AIR LVIII Happy groves

O cruel, cruel, cruel case!
Must I suffer this disgrace?

55. *particular:* exact and detailed.

56. In this scene Macheath sings fragments of nine different melodies before ending with his Air to the tune of 'Greensleeves'; this parodies the operatic technique of recitative modulating into aria.

AIR LIX Of all the girls that are so smart

Of all the friends in time of grief,
When threat'ning death looks grimmer,
Not one so sure can bring relief,
As this best friend, a brimmer.[57]   [*Drinks.*]

AIR LX Britons strike home

Since I must swing, – I scorn, I scorn to wince or whine.

                    [*Rises.*]

AIR LXI Chevy Chase

But now again my spirits sink;
I'll raise them high with wine.

           [*Drinks a glass of wine.*]

AIR LXII To old Sir Simon the King

But valour the stronger grows,
The stronger liquor we're drinking.
And how can we feel our woes,
When we've lost the trouble of thinking?

             [*Drinks.*]

AIR LXIII Joy to great Caesar

If thus – A man can die
Much bolder with brandy.

         [*Pours out a bumper of brandy.*]

AIR LXIV There was an old woman

So I drink off this bumper. And now I can stand the test.
And my comrades shall see, that I die as brave as the best.

             [*Drinks.*]

57. *brimmer*: a glass filled to the brim.

AIR LXV *Did you ever hear of a gallant sailor*

> *But can I leave my pretty hussies,*
> *Without one tear, or tender sigh?*

AIR LXVI *Why are mine eyes still flowing*

> *Their eyes, their lips, their busses[58]*
> *Recall my love. Ah must I die!*

AIR LXVII *Green sleeves*

> *Since laws were made for every degree,*
> *To curb vice in others, as well as me,*
> *I wonder we han't better company,*
> *Upon Tyburn Tree!*
> *But gold from law can take out the sting;*
> *And if rich men like us were to swing,*
> *'Twould thin the land, such numbers to string*
> *Upon Tyburn Tree!*

JAILOR: Some friends of yours, Captain, desire to be admitted. I leave you together.

SCENE XIV

MACHEATH, BEN BUDGE, MATT OF THE MINT

MACHEATH: For my having broke prison, you see, gentlemen, I am ordered immediate execution. The Sheriff's Officers, I believe, are now at the door. That Jemmy Twitcher should peach me, I own surprised me! 'Tis a plain proof that the world is all alike, and that even our gang can no more trust one another than other people. Therefore, I beg you, gentlemen, look well to yourselves, for in all probability you may live some months longer.

58. *busses:* kisses.

MATT OF THE MINT: We are heartily sorry, Captain, for your misfortune. But 'tis what we must all come to.

MACHEATH: Peachum and Lockit, you know, are infamous scoundrels. Their lives are as much in your power,[59] as yours are in theirs. Remember your dying friend! 'Tis my last request. Bring those villains to the gallows before you, and I am satisfied.

MATT OF THE MINT: We'll do't.

JAILOR: Miss Polly and Miss Lucy entreat a word with you.

MACHEATH: Gentlemen, adieu.

SCENE XV

LUCY, MACHEATH, POLLY

MACHEATH: My dear Lucy. My dear Polly. Whatsoever hath passed between us is now at an end. If you are fond of marrying[60] again, the best advice I can give you, is to ship yourselves off for the West Indies,[61] where you'll have a fair chance of getting a husband apiece; or by good luck, two or three, as you like best.

POLLY: How can I support this sight!

LUCY: There is nothing moves one so much as a great man in distress.

AIR LXVIII All you that must take a leap

LUCY:	*Would I might be hanged!*
POLLY:	*And I would so too!*
LUCY:	*To be hanged with you.*

59. *Their lives . . . power:* i.e. the members of the gang have enough evidence to hang Peachum and Lockit, should they wish to do so, though the reverse is also the case.

60. *fond of marrying:* eager to marry.

61. *ship yourselves . . . Indies:* paupers often indentured themselves as servants in the American colonies. In *Polly*, the sequel to *The Beggar's Opera*, Polly does indeed travel to the West Indies and finds a husband there.

POLLY: *My dear, with you.*

MACHEATH: *O leave me to thought! I fear! I doubt!*
             I tremble! I droop! See, my courage is out.

                              [*Turns up the empty bottle.*]

POLLY: *No token of love?*

MACHEATH: *See, my courage is out.*

                              [*Turns up the empty pot.*]

LUCY: *No token of love?*

POLLY: *Adieu.*

LUCY: *Farewell.*

MACHEATH: *But hark! I hear the toll of the bell.*[62]

CHORUS: *Tol de rol lol, etc.*

JAILOR: Four women more, Captain, with a child apiece! See,
here they come. [*Enter women and children.*]

MACHEATH: What – four wives more! This is too much. Here
– tell the Sheriff's Officers I am ready. [*Exit* MACHEATH
guarded.]

SCENE XVI

To them, enter PLAYER *and* BEGGAR

PLAYER: But, honest friend, I hope you don't intend that
Macheath shall be really executed.

BEGGAR: Most certainly, sir. To make the piece perfect, I was
for doing strict poetical justice.[63] Macheath is to be hanged;
and for the other personages of the drama, the audience
must have supposed they were all either hanged or transported.

62. *toll of the bell:* the bell of St Sepulchre's Church, near Newgate, began to ring about
five minutes before condemned criminals left the prison to be taken to Tyburn for
execution.

63. *poetical justice:* the doctrine that, in order to reflect the just nature of God's universe,
drama ought to show wickedness punished and virtue rewarded; see editors' introduction, p. 29.

PLAYER: Why then, friend, this is a downright deep tragedy. The catastrophe is manifestly wrong, for an opera must end happily.

BEGGAR: Your objection, sir, is very just; and is easily removed. For you must allow, that in this kind of drama, 'tis no matter how absurdly things are brought about.[64] So – you rabble there – run and cry a reprieve – let the prisoner be brought back to his wives in triumph.

PLAYER: All this we must do, to comply with the taste of the town.

BEGGAR: Through the whole piece you may observe such a similitude of manners in high and low life, that it is difficult to determine whether (in the fashionable vices) the fine gentlemen imitate the gentlemen of the road, or the gentlemen of the road the fine gentlemen. Had the play remained, as I at first intended, it would have carried a most excellent moral. 'Twould have shown that the lower sort of people have their vices in a degree as well as the rich: and that they are punished for them.

SCENE XVII

To them, MACHEATH *with rabble, etc.*

MACHEATH: So, it seems, I am not left to my choice,[65] but must have a wife at last. Look ye, my dears, we will have no controversy now. Let us give this day to mirth, and I am sure she who thinks herself my wife will testify her joy by a dance.

ALL: Come, a dance – a dance.

64. *an opera . . . brought about:* the plots of Italian opera customarily ended happily, often at the cost of considerable violence to the laws of probability and logic; see editors' introduction, p. 9.

65. *I am not left to my choice:* i.e. to be hanged rather than marry – cf. III.xv.

MACHEATH: Ladies, I hope you will give me leave to present a partner to each of you. And (if I may without offence) for this time, I take Polly for mine. [*To* POLLY.] And for life, you slut, for we were really married. As for the rest . . . But at present keep your own secret.

A DANCE

AIR LXIX Lumps of pudding

Thus I stand like the Turk, with his doxies around;[66]
From all sides their glances his passion confound;
For black, brown, and fair, his inconstancy burns,
And the different beauties subdue him by turns:
Each calls forth her charms, to provoke his desires:
Though willing to all; with but one he retires.
But think of this maxim, and put off your sorrow,
The wretch of today, may be happy tomorrow.

CHORUS: *But think of this maxim, etc.*

FINIS

66. *the Turk*: the Sultan of Turkey, who maintained a large harem of slave women; *doxies*: wenches, whores.

READ MORE IN PENGUIN

In every corner of the world, on every subject under the sun, Penguin represents quality and variety – the very best in publishing today.

For complete information about books available from Penguin – including Puffins, Penguin Classics and Arkana – and how to order them, write to us at the appropriate address below. Please note that for copyright reasons the selection of books varies from country to country.

In the United Kingdom: Please write to *Dept. EP, Penguin Books Ltd, Bath Road, Harmondsworth, West Drayton, Middlesex UB7 ODA*

In the United States: Please write to *Consumer Sales, Penguin USA, P.O. Box 999, Dept. 17109, Bergenfield, New Jersey 07621-0120*. VISA and MasterCard holders call 1-800-253-6476 to order Penguin titles

In Canada: Please write to *Penguin Books Canada Ltd, 10 Alcorn Avenue, Suite 300, Toronto, Ontario M4V 3B2*

In Australia: Please write to *Penguin Books Australia Ltd, P.O. Box 257, Ringwood, Victoria 3134*

In New Zealand: Please write to *Penguin Books (NZ) Ltd, Private Bag 102902, North Shore Mail Centre, Auckland 10*

In India: Please write to *Penguin Books India Pvt Ltd, 706 Eros Apartments, 56 Nehru Place, New Delhi 110 019*

In the Netherlands: Please write to *Penguin Books Netherlands bv, Postbus 3507, NL-1001 AH Amsterdam*

In Germany: Please write to *Penguin Books Deutschland GmbH, Metzlerstrasse 26, 60594 Frankfurt am Main*

In Spain: Please write to *Penguin Books S. A., Bravo Murillo 19, 1° B, 28015 Madrid*

In Italy: Please write to *Penguin Italia s.r.l., Via Felice Casati 20, I–20124 Milano*

In France: Please write to *Penguin France S. A., 17 rue Lejeune, F–31000 Toulouse*

In Japan: Please write to *Penguin Books Japan, Ishikiribashi Building, 2–5–4, Suido, Bunkyo-ku, Tokyo 112*

In South Africa: Please write to *Longman Penguin Southern Africa (Pty) Ltd, Private Bag X08, Bertsham 2013*

READ MORE IN PENGUIN

A CHOICE OF CLASSICS

Francis Bacon	**The Essays**
Aphra Behn	**Love-Letters between a Nobleman and His Sister**
	Oroonoko, The Rover and Other Works
George Berkeley	**Principles of Human Knowledge/Three Dialogues between Hylas and Philonous**
James Boswell	**The Life of Samuel Johnson**
Sir Thomas Browne	**The Major Works**
John Bunyan	**The Pilgrim's Progress**
Edmund Burke	**Reflections on the Revolution in France**
Frances Burney	**Evelina**
Margaret Cavendish	**The Blazing World and Other Writings**
William Cobbett	**Rural Rides**
William Congreve	**Comedies**
Thomas de Quincey	**Confessions of an English Opium Eater**
	Recollections of the Lakes and the Lake Poets
Daniel Defoe	**A Journal of the Plague Year**
	Moll Flanders
	Robinson Crusoe
	Roxana
	A Tour Through the Whole Island of Great Britain
Henry Fielding	**Amelia**
	Jonathan Wild
	Joseph Andrews
	The Journal of a Voyage to Lisbon
	Tom Jones
John Gay	**The Beggar's Opera**
Oliver Goldsmith	**The Vicar of Wakefield**
Lady Gregory	**Selected Writings**

READ MORE IN PENGUIN

A CHOICE OF CLASSICS

William Hazlitt	**Selected Writings**
George Herbert	**The Complete English Poems**
Thomas Hobbes	**Leviathan**
Samuel Johnson/	
James Boswell	**A Journey to the Western Islands of Scotland** and **The Journal of a Tour of the Hebrides**
Charles Lamb	**Selected Prose**
George Meredith	**The Egoist**
Thomas Middleton	**Five Plays**
John Milton	**Paradise Lost**
Samuel Richardson	**Clarissa**
	Pamela
Earl of Rochester	**Complete Works**
Richard Brinsley	
Sheridan	**The School for Scandal and Other Plays**
Sir Philip Sidney	**Selected Poems**
Christopher Smart	**Selected Poems**
Adam Smith	**The Wealth of Nations** (Books I–III)
Tobias Smollett	**The Adventures of Ferdinand Count Fathom**
	Humphrey Clinker
	Roderick Random
Laurence Sterne	**The Life and Opinions of Tristram Shandy**
	A Sentimental Journey Through France and Italy
Jonathan Swift	**Gulliver's Travels**
	Selected Poems
Thomas Traherne	**Selected Poems and Prose**
Henry Vaughan	**Complete Poems**